EMMA

Volume 9

By Kaoru Mori

Contents

Chapter 7 Erich and Theo........................003

Chapter 8 On Wings of Song....................037

Chapter 9 Friendship..................................071

Chapter 10 Shopping Together.................105

Chapter 11 Three Singers (part one).........139

Chapter 12 Three Singers (part two)........173

Afterword...207

CHAPTER 7: ERICH AND THEO

(ALL SQUARE BALLOONS DENOTE GERMAN)

HERE, THEO.
IT'S AN ACORN.

FATHER!
ACORNS!
WELL, WELL ...

THE FRUITCAKE WAS DELICIOUS.
LET'S SERVE IT AT OUR NEXT PARTY.
YES, MA'AM.

AH! LOOK!
THERE ARE A LOT ON THE GROUND OVER HERE.
FATHER ...
... CAN WE BRING ACORNS HOME?
ONLY A FEW.

WELL ...

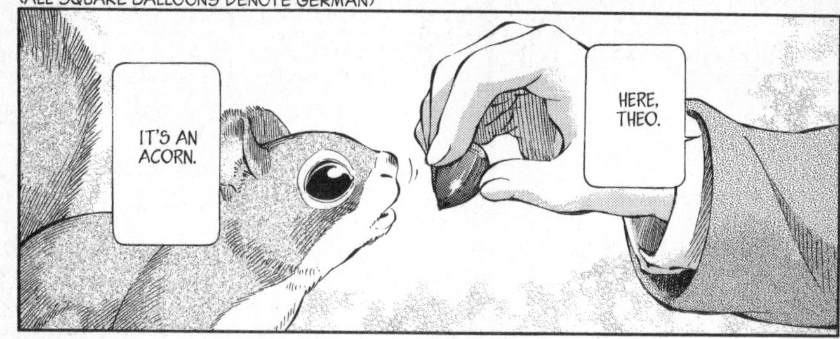

CHAPTER 7: ERICH AND THEO
I THINK IT'S TIME, DARLING.
IT'S TIME, ERICH AND ILSE.
WE'RE GOING HOME NOW.
OKAY...
DON'T BICKER WITH ME, THEO.
CHI CHI
IF YOU DON'T GO IN THE BOX, YOU CAN'T COME BACK HOME WITH US.

MOTHER! MOTHER!
WHAT IS IT, ERICH?

WE'RE LEAVING ALREADY?
IT'LL BE PITCH BLACK BY THE TIME WE ARRIVE HOME.

SHIVER

ER...
I, UH...

MADAME...
I'LL TAKE HIM.
OH, YES, PLEASE.

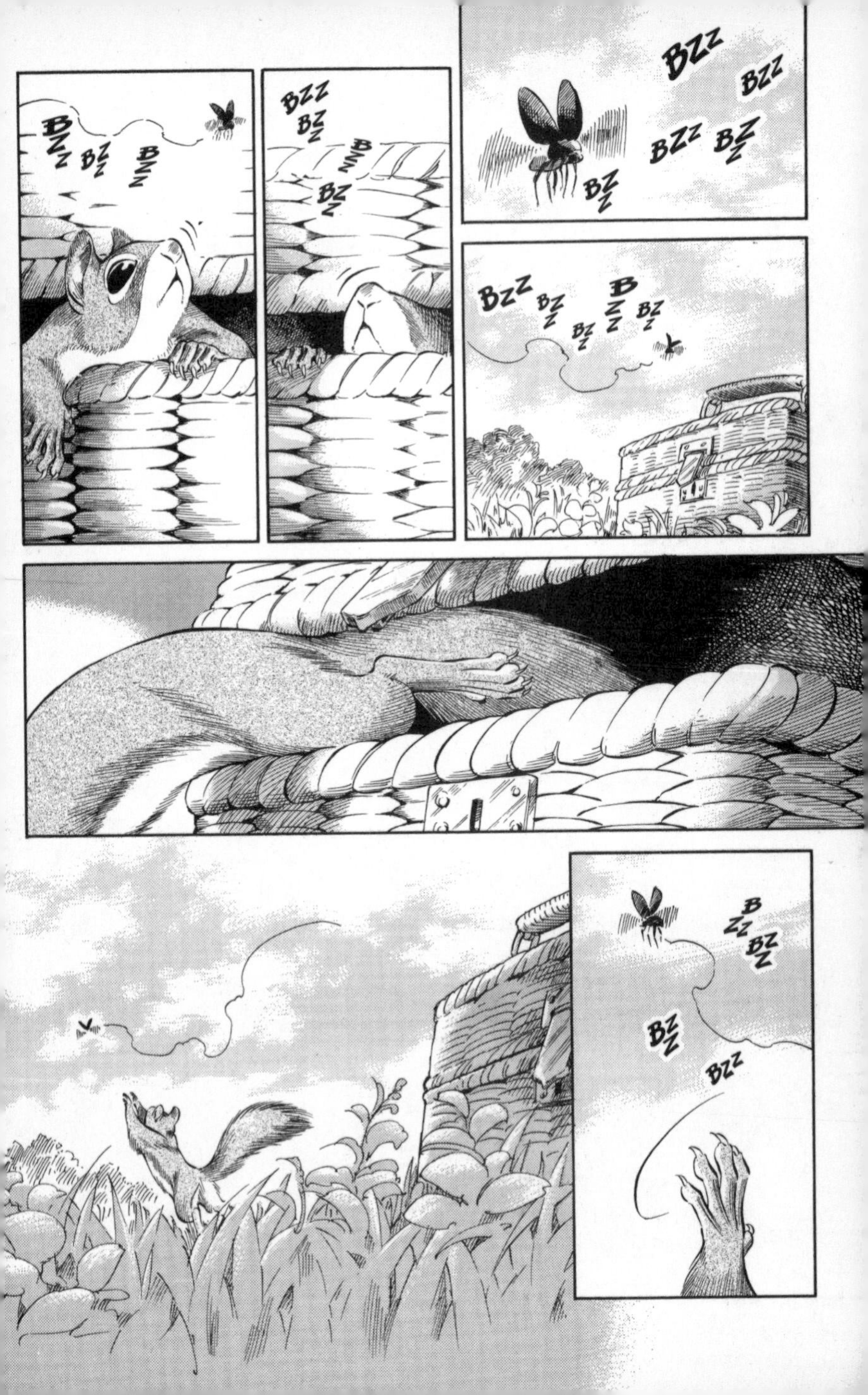
BZZ
BZZ
BZZ
BZZ
BZZ
BZZ
BZZ
BZZ
BZZ
BZZ
BZZ
BZZ
BZZ
BZZ
BZZ
BZZ
BZZ
BZZ
BZZ
BZZ
BZZ
BZZ
BZZ

DID YOU WASH YOUR HANDS?
YES!

THEN WE'RE GOING.
HURRY UP AND GET ON BOARD.

COMING!

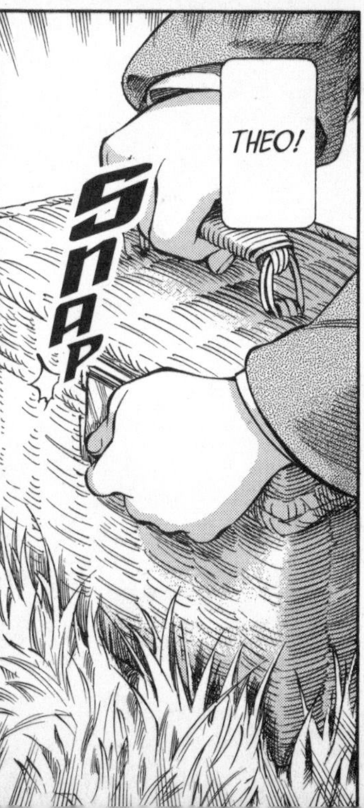
THEO!
SNAP

CHIII
CHIII

RATTLE
RATTLE
CLATTER

CLATTER
CLATTER

ASLEEP ALREADY?

THEY'RE WORN OUT FROM PLAYING.

EVEN THEO IS QUIET.

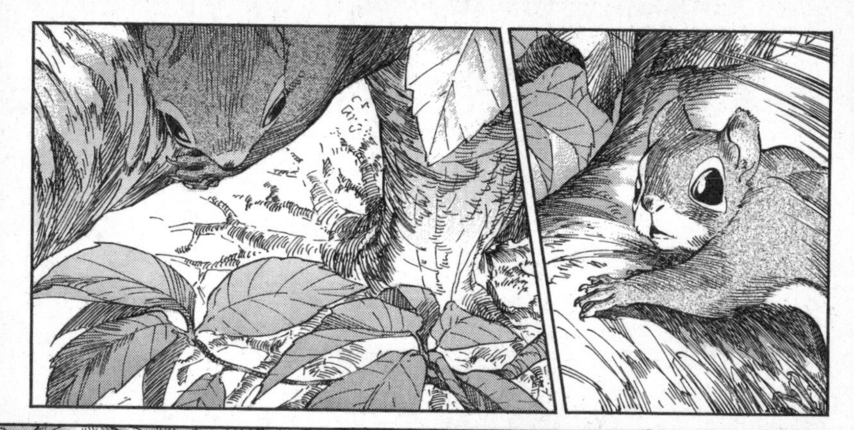

TEK
TEK
TEK

RUSTLE
NIBBLE
NIBBLE
NIBBLE
NIBBLE
NIBBLE
NIBBLE
RUSTLE
RUSTLE
NIBBLE

SWISH
SWISH
PTOO
TA
TA
TA

KRKK
KKRK
SNAP
PATTER
PATTER
PATTER
SPLASH

CHIIII
AHCHOO
SCRATCH
SCRATCH
SCRATCH
SCRATCH

ERICH ...
WE'VE ARRIVED. ERICH...

MMM ...
I WANT YOU TO GO STRAIGHT TO BED.

COME ALONG, ERICH.
MM ...

DID YOU HAVE A GOOD TIME?

UH-HUH! A GREAT TIME!
VERY GOOD.

THEO ...
WE'RE HOME!

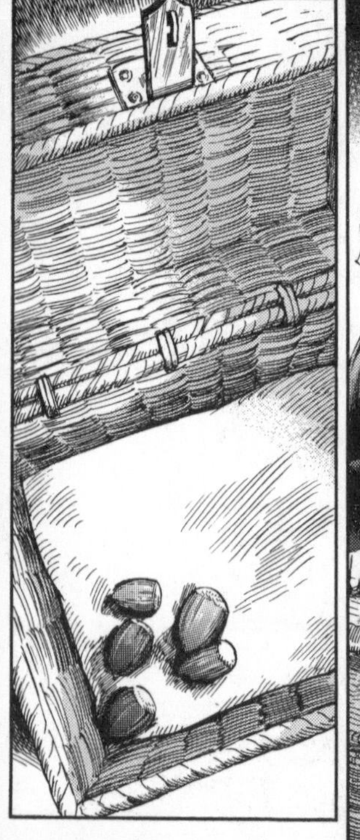

THEO'S GONE?!
THEO?!
WHAT? WHAT'S WRONG?
WAS HE IN THE WAGON?
THEO!
THEO!
ALL I KNOW ...
...IS THAT BY THE TIME WE ARRIVED, HE WAS MISSING.
I MUST HAVE LEFT HIM THERE...
I LEFT HIM THERE ...!
LET'S GO BACK !!
I'VE GOT TO FIND HIM!!

THEO...
THEO...
I LEFT THEO IN THE WOODS !!
I HAVE TO LOOK FOR HIM!!

I UNDER-STAND YOUR CONCERN...
...BUT CALM DOWN!
ERICH!
IM-POSSIBLE, IT'S TOO DARK NOW!
WE'LL GO BACK TOMOR-ROW.
NO, IT HAS TO BE NOW!
THEO...
THEO WILL...!!

BUT, THEO...
THEO IS A SQUIRREL, SO I'M SURE HE'LL FIND A SAFE PLACE TO HIDE FOR THE NIGHT.

THAT AREA IS DANGER-OUS AT NIGHT.
WHAT GOOD WILL IT DO ANYONE IF YOU GET LOST OR BREAK A LEG THERE?

IT'LL BE ALL RIGHT.
I'M SURE WE'LL FIND HIM.

WHEN IT GETS LIGHT, I'LL GO WITH YOU TO SEARCH.
FAIR ENOUGH?

SWOOP...

!!
FLAP
FLAP

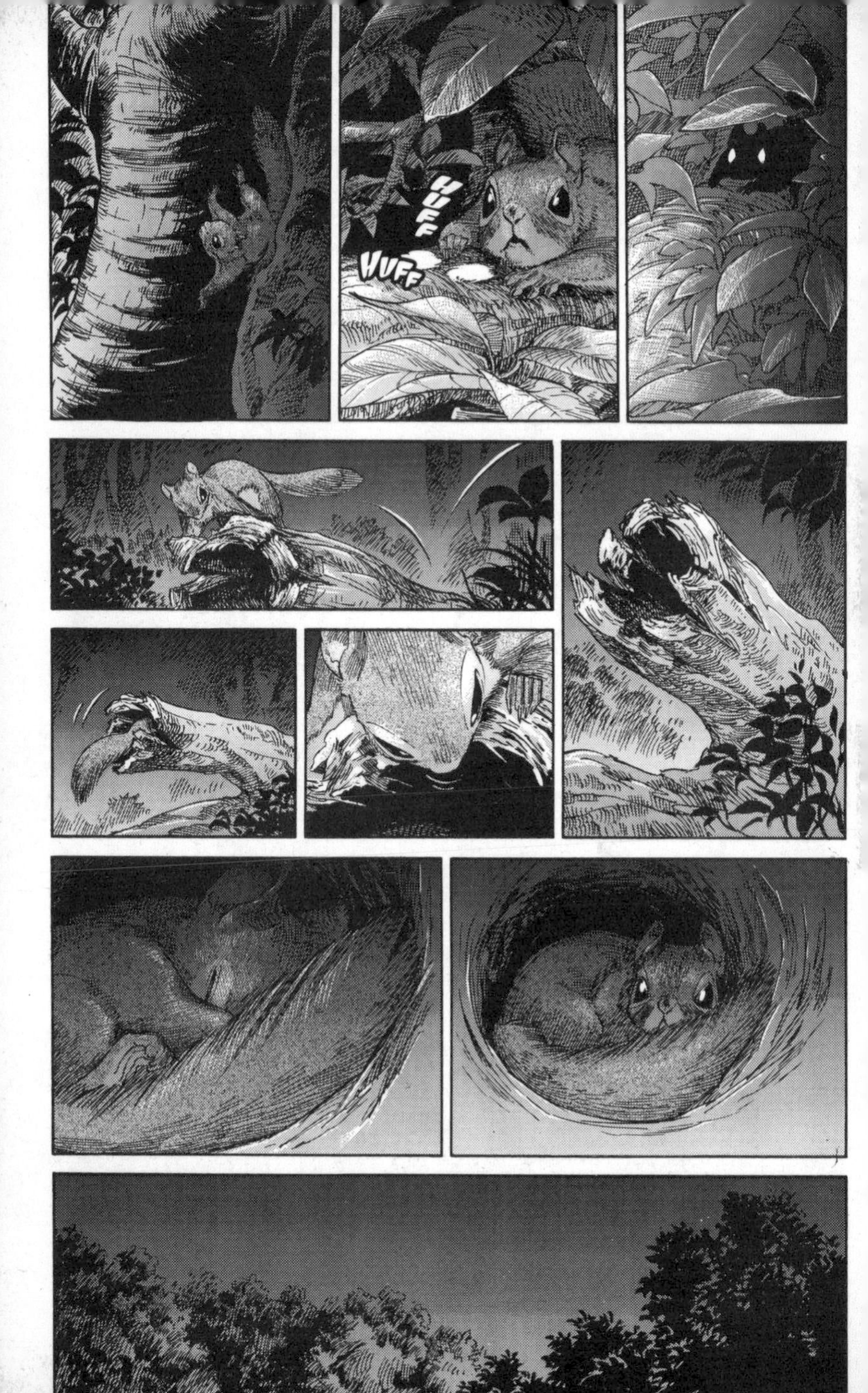
HUFF
HUFF

SCRATCH
SCRATCH
SCRATCH

THEO!!
THEO!!

THEO!!
TIME TO EAT! COME OUT!
RATTLE RATTLE RATTLE

ODD. THAT TRICK ALWAYS WORKS...
WHAT ARE THESE? WALNUTS?
HE PROBABLY CAN'T HEAR YOU.

THEO !!

THEO!!
IS HE THERE?!
THEO!
DO YOU SEE HIM?!
THEO!
COME HERE!!
THEO!!

THEO...
HAS HE BEEN FOUND?
IT SEEMS SO.
GOOD FOR YOU, YOUNG MASTER!
NOW WE CAN GO HOME!
Whew!
WHAT'S WRONG?
THEO URINATED ON ME.
OH, DEAR!
NO, NO, THEO!
YOU DON'T DO THAT!
IT MUST MEAN HE'S RELIEVED.

MAYBE HE'S BEEN HOLDING IT ALL THIS TIME...

THEO...

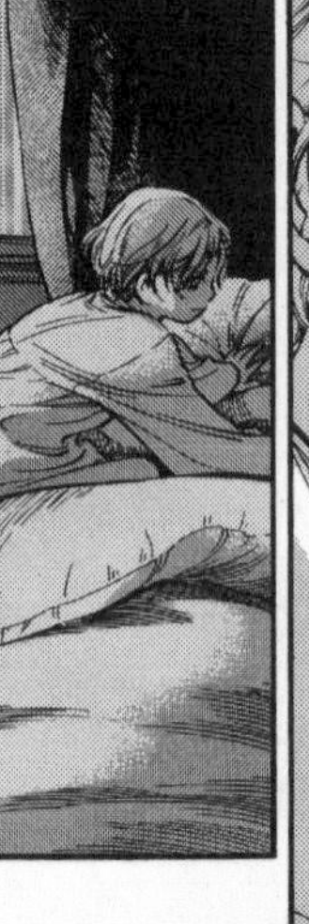

CHAPTER 8: ON WINGS OF SONG

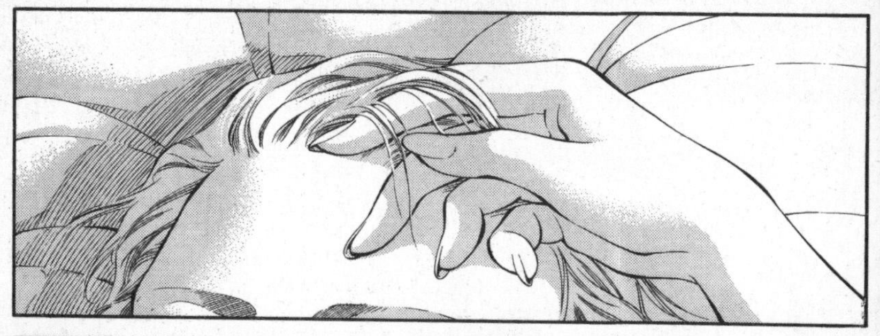

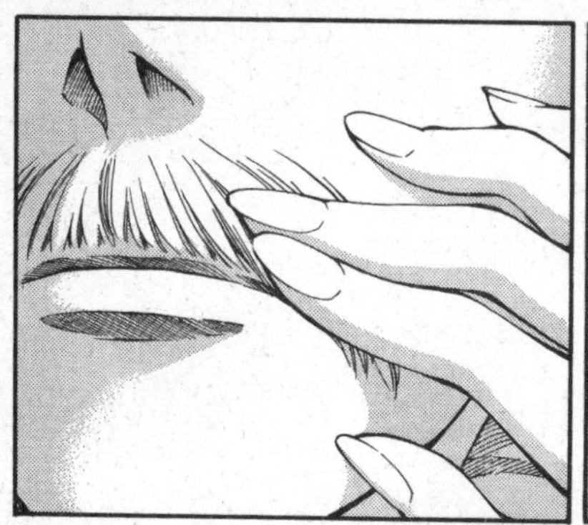

CHAPTER 8: ON THE WINGS OF SONG
GOOD MORNING, WILHELM.
GOOD MORNING.

WHAT TIME IS IT?

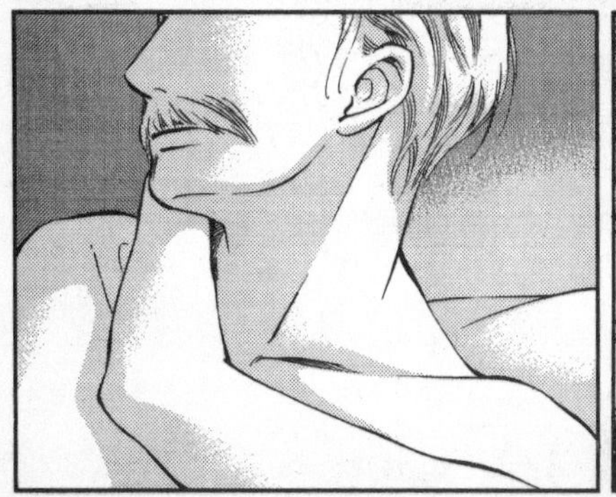

NOT TIME TO GET UP YET.
I JUST WOKE YOU UP BECAUSE I WAS AWAKE.

I HAD A PECULIAR DREAM.

A DREAM?
WHAT ABOUT?
....

I... HUH.
IT'S ALREADY ESCAPED ME.
OH.

HAS BRUCH COME?
NO.
THEN IT'S BEFORE NINE.

NINE O'CLOCK.
NOK NOK NOK
COME IN.

DARJEE-LING.
IT'S A LITTLE STRONG.

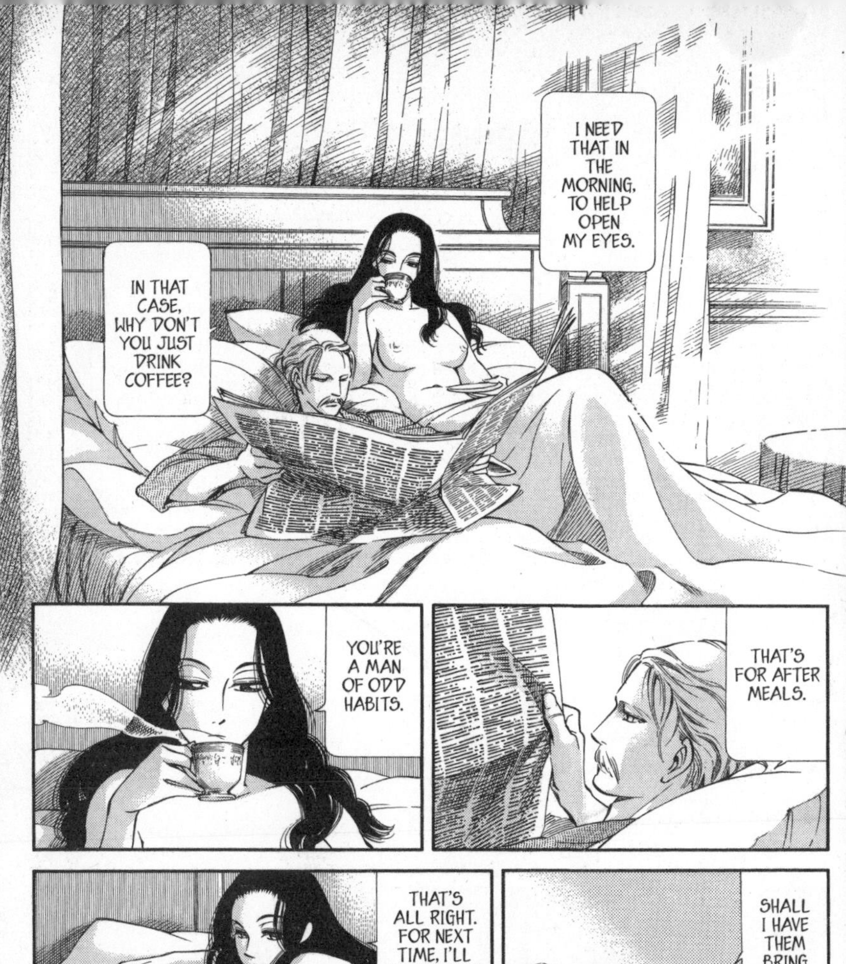
I NEED THAT IN THE MORNING, TO HELP OPEN MY EYES.
IN THAT CASE, WHY DON'T YOU JUST DRINK COFFEE?

THAT'S FOR AFTER MEALS.
YOU'RE A MAN OF ODD HABITS.
SHALL I HAVE THEM BRING THE TRAY FROM YOUR ROOM OVER?
WHEN I STAY HERE, I DON'T ORDER A MORNING TRAY.
THAT'S ALL RIGHT. FOR NEXT TIME, I'LL ASK THEM TO BRING A POT OF HOT WATER.
ANY INTERESTING ARTICLES?
NO.

IT'S A PAIN HAVING SEPARATE ROOMS.
WHY DON'T WE GO BACK TO SHARING SOON?

OH, THIS WAY SUITS ME.
I DON'T WANT YOU TO SEE ME PUTTING ON MAKEUP.

OR DO YOU WANT TO WATCH ME DO THAT?
NOT PARTI-CULAR-LY.
SEE?

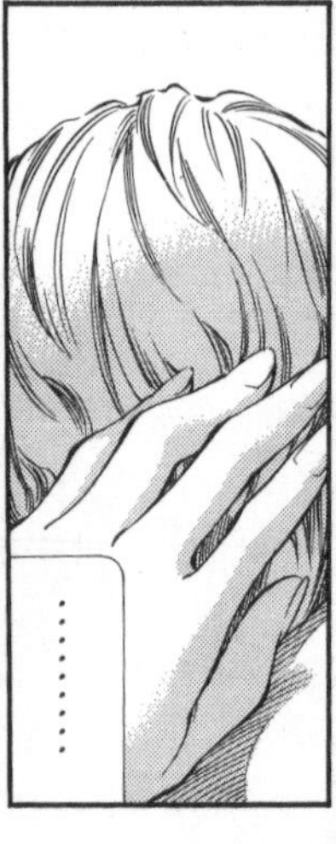
....

WHITE HAIR.
......

......

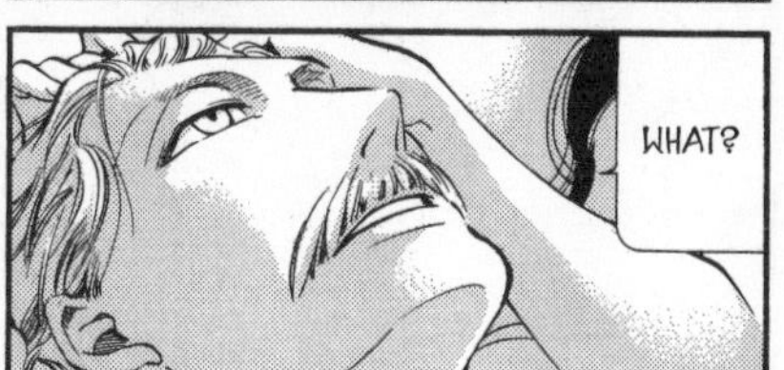
WHAT?

WITH THE COLOR OF YOUR HAIR...
...IT DOESN'T STAND OUT AT ALL.
THAT'S ALL RIGHT.

...THE DEVIL, YOU SAY!

BUT IF I'M GOING TO, I WANT THEM TO BE PURE WHITE.
I DON'T LIKE GRAY.

DO YOU HAVE ANY, DOROTHEA?
NO.
NOT YET, AT LEAST.

MY GRAND-AUNT'S HAIR TURNED SNOW WHITE.
WITH WHITE HAIR, YOU CAN WEAR A DRESS OF ANY COLOR.

THAT WOULD BE DIS-APPOINT-ING...

I LIKE BLACK HAIR.
YOU ALWAYS HAVE.

IS THAT WHY YOU MARRIED ME, FOR MY BLACK HAIR?

OR DID YOU FALL IN LOVE WITH ME BECAUSE I HAD BLACK HAIR?

I MARRIED YOU FOR YOUR BLACK HAIR.

KEEP IT UP WITH THOSE JOKES.
WHAT WOULD YOU DO IF I HAD AN AFFAIR?

DON'T.

...I WON'T.
GOOD.

YOU'RE IMPOSSIBLE.
IN WHAT WAY?

MOST OF THE TIME, I CAN'T TELL WHETHER YOU'RE JOKING OR SERIOUS.
EVER SINCE THEN...

SINCE WHEN?
THE FIRST TIME WE MET.

YOU REMEMBER, DON'T YOU? AT SOME PARTY.

IF A FELLOW WALKED IN FRONT OF YOU ABSENT-MINDEDLY, I BET HE WOULD BE KICKED OUT OF THE WAY.

WHILE LOOKING AT MY FACE, YOU SAID...

NO...
WE MET ONCE BEFORE THAT.

I THOUGHT, "WHAT KIND OF THING IS THAT TO SAY FOR A FIRST MEETING?"

WHERE?
A PATH.

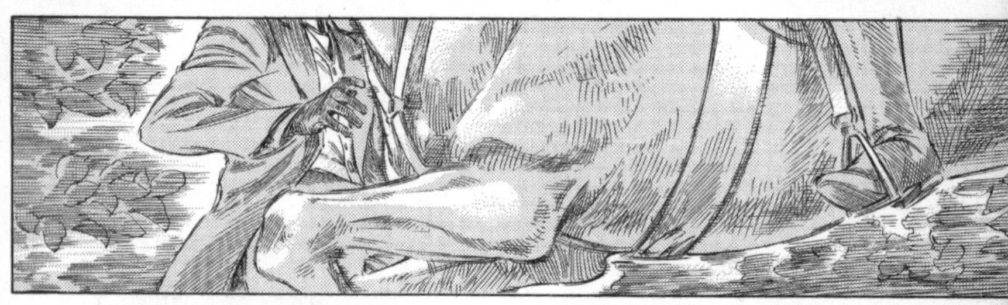

YOU NEARLY RAN ME OVER.

I'M SORRY!

STRADDLING A MAN'S SADDLE, WITH YOUR HAIR UNBOUND...
...I THOUGHT TO MYSELF, "WHAT A ROUGH YOUNG WOMAN."

YOU OFTEN RODE A HORSE BACK THEN.
TO REDUCE STRESS.
THERE WERE MANY THINGS I DIDN'T CARE FOR AT THE TIME.

YOU NEVER MENTIONED THAT ENCOUNTER BEFORE.

I KNEW I'D SEEN YOUR FACE SOMEWHERE BEFORE.

...BECAUSE YOU HAD SUCH A COMPOSED EXPRESSION.

AT FIRST, I COULDN'T PLACE YOU...

HENCE THE STARING.

ANOTHER JEST?
WHY NOT?

YOU WERE MORE FASCINATING ON THE PATH THAN AT THE PARTY.

WELL, I COULDN'T VERY WELL HAVE RIDDEN A HORSE TO A SOIREE, COULD I HAVE?

WAS IT THE HAIR?
IT WAS THE HAIR.

YOU KNOW, ONCE IN A WHILE, YOU SAY THINGS THAT DON'T MAKE SENSE.
I DO?
WHEN?

REMEMBER WHEN I CAME TO ASK YOUR HAND IN MARRIAGE?
I ASKED IF THERE WAS ANYTHING I COULD DO FOR YOU.

WOULD YOU GROW A MOUSTACHE?

I THOUGHT IT A STRANGE REQUEST.

CERTAINLY, I WAS AT THE AGE WHERE A MOUSTACHE WOULDN'T LOOK OUT OF PLACE...
...AND IF YOU HAD AN AFFINITY FOR THEM, WELL...

THAT WAS...

...DON'T PARTICULARLY CARE ABOUT FACIAL HAIR ONE WAY OR THE OTHER.

YOU MAY NOT REALIZE THIS, DARLING...
...BUT YOU'VE GOT A SCARY FACE.

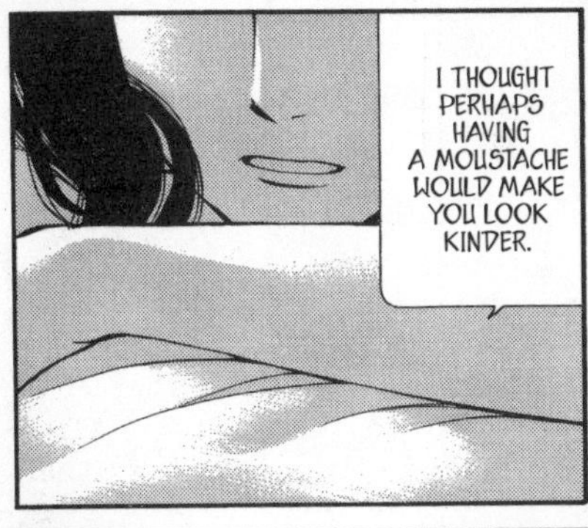
I THOUGHT PERHAPS HAVING A MOUSTACHE WOULD MAKE YOU LOOK KINDER.

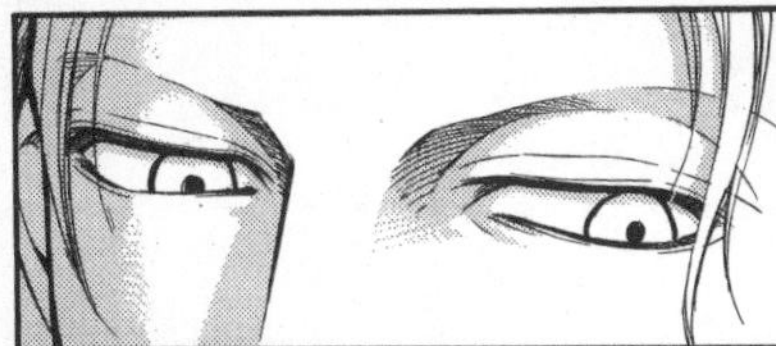

A SCARY FACE?
BACK THEN.

NOT NOW?
OF COURSE NOT.

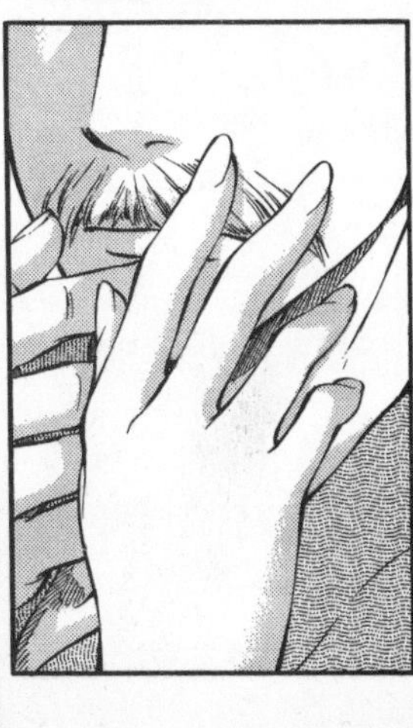

I NEVER THOUGHT YOU WOULD ACTUALLY GROW ONE FOR ME.

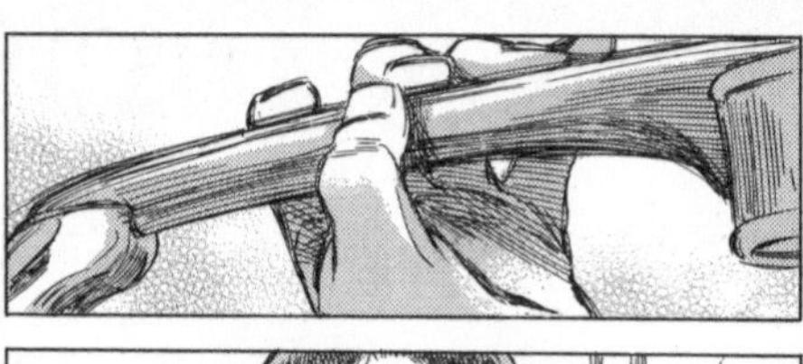

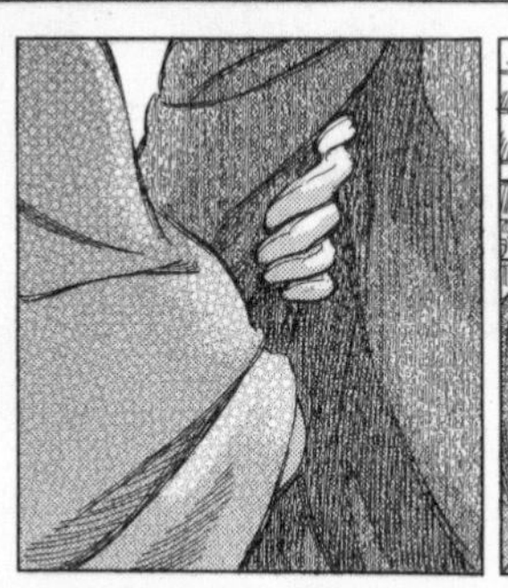

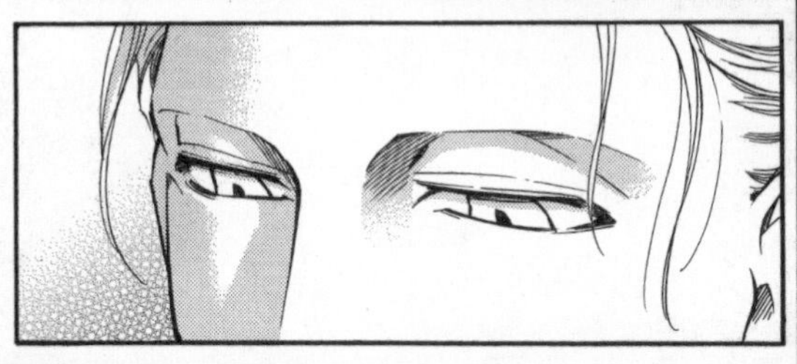

SAY...
HOW MANY YEARS HAVE WE BEEN MARRIED?

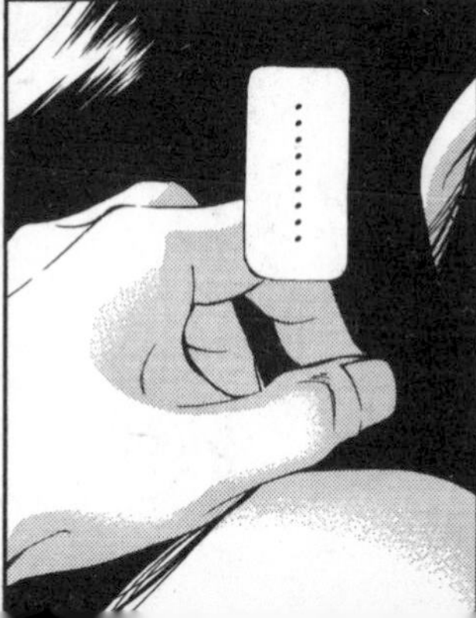
....

EIGHT AND A HALF.
REALLY?
THAT LONG?

CURIOUS, HOW TIME FLIES.
YOU'RE A WONDERFUL MAN, AFTER ALL.

DARLING...
SING ME SOME-THING.

A SONG?
YES. SING ME A SONG.

SING WHAT?
ANY-THING.

....

Auf Flügeln des Gesanges,
(ON WINGS OF SONG...)
Herzliebchen, trag
(...I'LL CARRY...)
ich dich fort,
(...YOU AWAY...)
Fort nach den Fluren
(...FAR AWAY...)
des Ganges,
(...TO THE FIELDS OF THE GANGES...)
Dort weiss ich den
(...TO THAT PLACE...)
schönsten Ort;
(...THAT I KNOW.)
Dort liegt ein rotblühender Garten
(THERE LIES A RED, FLOWERING GARDEN...)
Im stillen Mondenschein,
(...IN THE STILL MOONLIGHT...)

Die Lotosblumen
(...WHERE THE LOTUS FLOWERS...)
erwarten
(...AWAIT YOU...)
Ihr trautes Schwesterlein.
(...THEIR BELOVED SISTER.)
Die Veilchen kichern
(THE VIOLETS CHUCKLE...)
und kosen,
(...AND FROLIC...)

Und schau'n nach den
(...AND WHISPER...)
Sternen empor,
(...AT THE DISTANT STARS...)
Heimlich erzählen die Rosen
E THE ROSES SURREPTITIOUSLY TELL...)
Sich duftende Märchen
(...SWEET-SMELLING FAIRY TALES...)
in's Ohr.
(...IN OUR EARS.)

Dort wollen wir——
(THERE WE WILL...)

wir niedersinken
(... WE WILL SIT DOWN...)
Unter dem Palmenbaum,
(...IN THE SHADE OF A PALM TREE...)

GO ON.
I LOVE THIS SONG.

Und Lieb' und——
(...AND YOU, MY LOVE...)

......

I CAN'T SING IF YOU KISS ME.

?

WAIT.

IT'S TOO BRIGHT IN HERE.

WILHELM ...?
MM?
I LOVE YOU.

CHAPTER 9: FRIENDSHIP

"SO THIS IS WHAT INDIA IS LIKE...", I THOUGHT.

CHAPTER 9: FRIEND-SHIP

WAIT HERE A MOMENT.

THIS WAY, PLEASE.

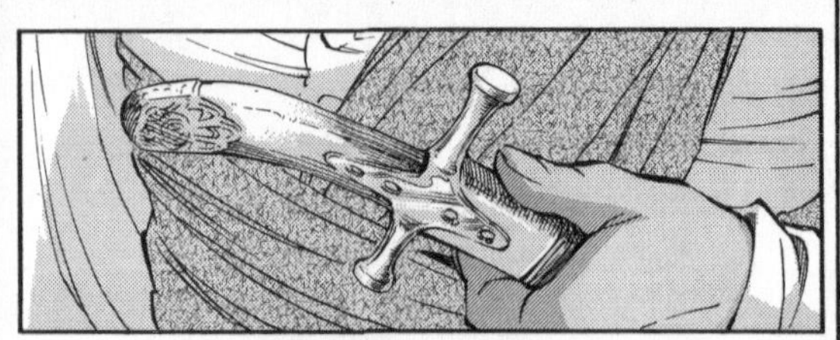

NO WORRIES.
THEY'RE BODY-GUARDS.

BODY-GUARDS?

THEIR DUTY IS TO PROTECT THE PRINCES.

....

I PRESENT THE SECOND PRINCE IN LINE TO THE THRONE ...
HIS HIGHNESS, HAKIM ATAWALLY.
AND THIS IS MASTER WILLIAM JONES.

IT SEEMS THAT HIS MAJESTY'S SECOND-OLDEST SON IS ABOUT THE SAME AGE AS WILLIAM.

YOU'RE GOING TO TAKE WILLIAM ALONG?

LUCKY! WHY DOES ONLY WILLIAM GET TO GO?

HIS MAJESTY WISHES TO HAVE HIS SON GET ACQUAINTED WITH ENGLAND WHILE HE'S STILL YOUNG.
AND IT WILL BE A GOOD OPPORTUNITY FOR WILLIAM TO LEARN ABOUT INDIA AS WELL.

PATIENCE, GRACE. WHEN YOU GET A LITTLE BIGGER, YOU'LL BE ABLE TO GO, TOO.
BUT THIS TIME, YOU AND I WILL WATCH THE HOUSE.

FATHER ...

CAN I TAKE THIS WITH, TOO?
LIMIT YOUR LUGGAGE TO THE NECESSITIES.

I'M GOING TO GIVE THIS TO THAT BOY.
I DIDN'T KNOW WHAT TO GIVE HIM FOR A PRESENT ...

...SO I WAS TOLD THAT SOMETHING WE COULD PLAY WITH TOGETHER MIGHT BE GOOD.
TOLD BY WHOM?
BY STEPHENS.

......

FINE.
THOUGH I CAN'T PROMISE THE CHILD WILL BE ABLE TO PLAY.
THANK YOU!

I DO HOPE WE CAN BECOME FRIENDS ...

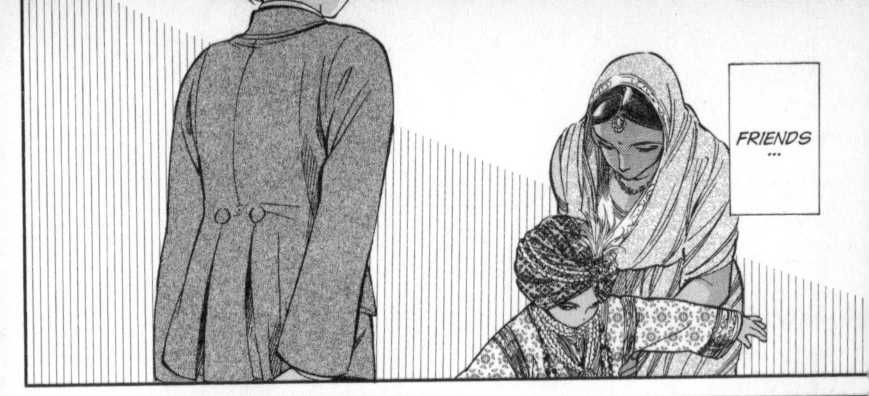
FRIENDS
...

IT--
IT'S A PLEASURE TO MEET YOU.

HE TALKED ...

THE PRINCE ASKED ME WHAT YOU SAID.

OH.

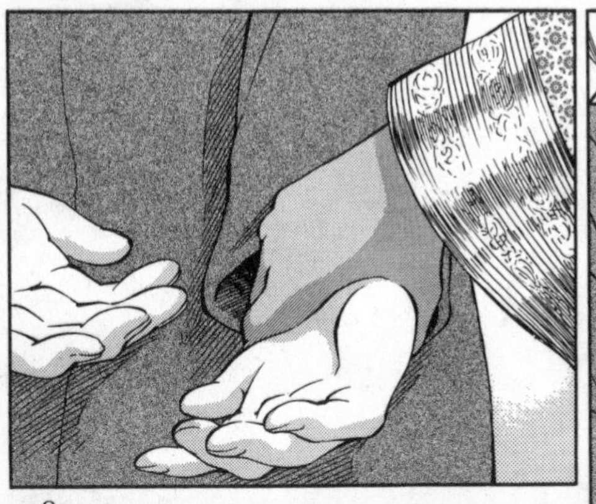

WHA--?!

......
AM I THAT UNUSUAL...?

?

ACK!
RIP

....
WHAT WAS THAT FOR...?!

HE SAYS YOUR BODY IS AS WHITE AS AN ELEPHANT'S TUSK.
IT'S A GREAT COMPLIMENT.

THE FABRICS HERE ARE IMMENSELY POPULAR, EVEN IN ENGLAND.
OUR LAST PRODUCT, TOO...

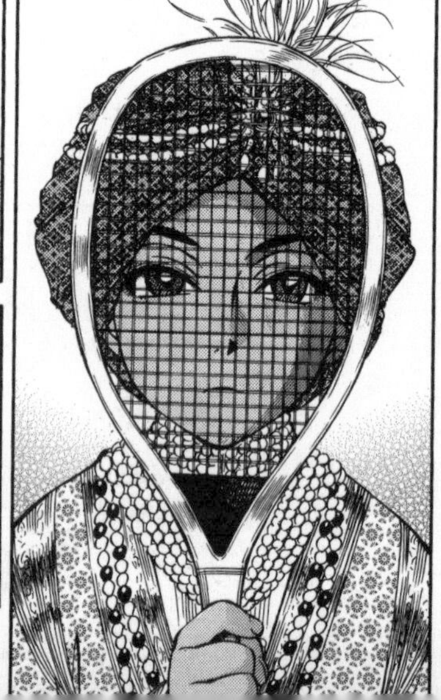

THIS GAME IS CALLED "TENNIS"...

HAVE YOU EVER PLAYED...
NO.
YOU HAVEN'T.

READY?
I'M GOING TO HIT THE BALL NOW.
WHOK

POK
POK
POK

ERM...
AFTER I HIT THE BALL ...
...YOU HIT IT BACK TO ME.
AND WE KEEP KNOCKING IT BACK AND FORTH. THAT'S THE GAME...
DO YOU UNDERSTAND?

ALL RIGHT, LET'S TRY IT AGAIN.
READY?

POK
WHOK
......

?

UM ...
HE SAYS ...

...THAT IF THE BALL DOESN'T COME TO HIM...
...HE'S NOT GOING TO HIT IT.

UH...
ALL RIGHT, THEN ...

THOOK

WHOK
WHOA!
?!
KRASH

AH...

WILLIAM!

READY?

KRSSSHH
KLANG
KRANG
CLATTER CLATTER

WHOK
AH!
WHOK
THAT'S IT!
JUST LIKE THAT !!
WHOK

YES, RIGHT AT ME!
WHOK
WELL DONE!
WHOK

EVEN THOUGH TODAY WAS HIS FIRST TIME...
... ALREADY HE CAN RETURN IT AND WITH GOOD AIM!

HE'S BRILLIANT AT IT!

HE WANTS TO PLAY AGAIN TOMOR-ROW!

I SEE ...

HIS MAJESTY HAS SAID THAT HE WISHES TO OBSERVE.
I BELIEVE THAT I'LL WATCH TOMORROW AS WELL.

GREAT!

AFTER YOU FINISHED YESTERDAY, HIS HIGHNESS ASKED ME VARIOUS QUESTIONS REGARDING TENNIS...
I was up all night researching.
......

WILLIAM!

WOW!
TENNIS CLOTHES ...

YES.
YOU HAD A COURT BUILT, TOO.

......

BUT I THINK IT MAY BE A BIT TOO BIG...

KLANK KLANK
KLANK

YES...
THAT SEEMS ABOUT RIGHT...

....

...ALL RIGHT.
I'M GOING TO HIT IT.

ARE THESE MATCHES HELD OFTEN IN ENGLAND?

SO ...
...I WAS ASKED.

YES, I SUPPOSE SO.
I BELIEVE IT'S A VERY POPULAR ACTIVITY.

IT RESEMBLES A CRICKET MATCH. HOW DOES IT DIFFER?

CRICKET IS PLAYED WITH TWO TEAMS.

TENNIS IS A SPORT WITH ONLY TWO OR FOUR PLAYERS ...
...USUALLY CLOSE FRIENDS WHO PLAY FOR ENJOYMENT.

AH!
WHOA!
MANY ENGLISHMEN HAVE COME TO VISIT, BUT THIS IS THE FIRST TIME I'VE SEEN THIS SPORT.
......
NO FOREIGN NATION HAS EVER GOVERNED INDIA FOR LONG.

YOUR COUNTRY IS, AS IT WERE, A TRAVELER PASSING THROUGH.
EVENTUALLY, YOU WILL LEAVE.
BUT AFTER YOUR SOJOURN IS OVER...
...HOW WILL YOU SEE US?
AS FRIENDS?
OR...

WHAT'S WRONG?
FINISHED ALREADY?
......
I LOST.

EVEN THOUGH IT WAS HIS FIRST MATCH ...

HAKIM!
LET'S PLAY AGAIN!

I AM NOT A SORE LOSER!
IN TENNIS, YOU PLAY SEVERAL GAMES IN A ROW, NOT JUST ONE!

BESIDES, THAT FIRST WAS ONLY PRACTICE!

......
IT APPEARS THAT AN INTERPRETER IS NO LONGER NEEDED.

I'M NOT LOSING THIS NEXT ONE!

WHOK
IN!!
AH!!
DRAT!!
I LOST!
I WON, WILLIAM!

OH, GRACE.
HELLO, ROBERT.
SO THOSE TWO WERE STILL PLAYING, EH?
TIED.
AND IN TOTAL?
WHO WON?
THE INDIAN FELLOW TOOK THIS LAST GAME.
THEY NEVER GET TIRED OF IT...

THEY BOTH PLAY AT ABOUT THE SAME LEVEL...
...AND THEY'VE GOT SIMILAR TEMPERA-MENTS.
SO THAT'S WHY THEY EACH WIN AS MUCH AS LOSE...
ALL RIGHT, ONE MORE GAME!!
THIS WILL SETTLE IT!!

ONE MORE?
LAST GAME!

LAST GAME...

ROBERT!
I HOPE THEY'LL LET ME PLAY TODAY...

WHOSE SERVICE?
WHOEVER HAS THE BALL CAN JUST HIT IT...
COME ON, ROBERT, TAKE THIS SERIOUSLY!

CHAPTER 10: SHOPPING TOGETHER

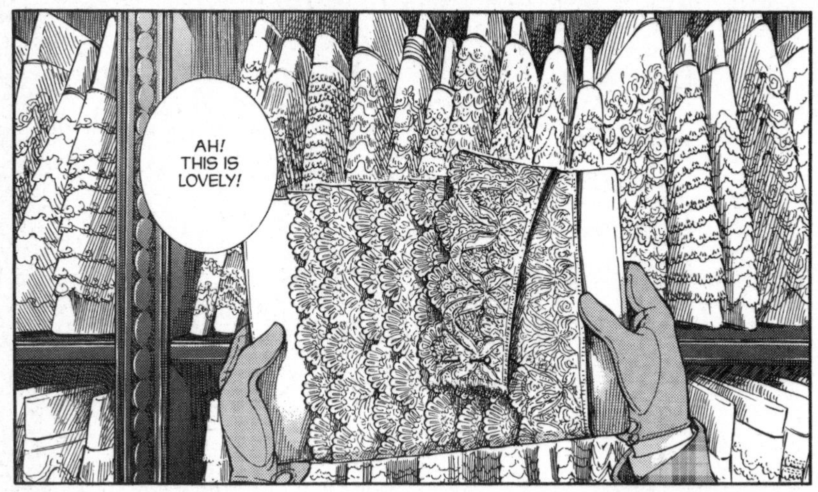
AH! THIS IS LOVELY!

SO DO YOU WORK IN THIS AREA?
NEAR HAWORTH, ACTUALLY.

EXCUSE ME.
DO YOU SELL THIS BY THE YARD?

I COULD SELL IT TO YOU BY THE FOOT, IF YOU LIKE.
HOW MUCH DO YOU WANT?

CHAPTER 10: SHOPPING TOGETHER
HOW MUCH WOULD SIX PENCE GET ME?
OF WHICH MATERIAL?

I DO HAVE SIMILAR MATERIAL THAT'S MACHINE-WOVEN ...
BUT THIS IS SO BEAUTI-FUL...

OH, THIS IS HAND-WOVEN, SO IT'S MORE EXPENSIVE.
You have keen eyes...
I'M AFRAID SIX PENCE WOULDN'T QUITE COVER IT.
AH...

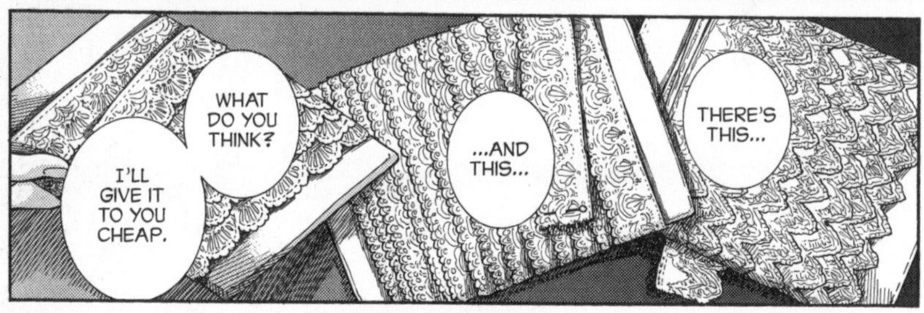
THERE'S THIS...
...AND THIS...
WHAT DO YOU THINK?
I'LL GIVE IT TO YOU CHEAP.

MMM ...

AFTER SEEING THIS ONE...
THERE'S NOTHING TO PONDER OVER.
ALL OF THE HAND-WOVEN MATERIAL IS TOO RICH FOR YOUR BLOOD.

SEEING OUR MISTRESS'S DRESSES HAS NEEDLESSLY MADE HER QUITE THE CONNOISSEUR.
I'D LIKE TO SELL YOU THE MATERIAL, AS YOU'RE SO OBVIOUSLY FOND OF IT...
...BUT I AM RUNNING A BUSINESS ...
MMM ....

HONESTLY
...

I SAID, IT'S RIGHT IN THIS AREA!!
YOU NEED TO BE MORE SPECIFIC!

ALMA!
WHAT'S GOING ON?

WHEN I TOLD THEM...
...THAT I'M GOING SHOPPING IN TOWN WITH YOU TOMORROW...
WHAT, YOU'RE GOING TOO, ALMA?
IN THAT CASE, MAYBE I'LL PUT IN A REQUEST AS WELL.

THERE'S SOMETHING THAT YOU WANT?
IF IT'S HEAVY, YOU CAN FORGET ABOUT IT.
DON'T WORRY. I JUST WANT...
...ONE SMALL PICTURE FRAME.

EH?! YOU'RE GOING TO BUY HER SOMETHING WHILE YOU'RE OUT?
CAN I ASK TOO, ALMA?
FINE, FINE.

FAIR WARNING, THOUGH. I DON'T KNOW THE SHOPS IN TOWN VERY WELL.
YOU'D DO BETTER TO ASK POLLY.
HOLD ON! ALMA!!

POLLY, WATCH WHAT I'M DRAWING!!
ALL RIGHT, ALL RIGHT...
YOU SEE?! IT'S HERE! RIGHT HERE!!
SKRITCH
SKRITCH

YOU'LL KNOW IT WHEN YOU SEE IT.
MM...
THE SHOP'S BUILDING IS BLUE!

EVERYONE HAD BETTER PAY ME BEFOREHAND...
...BECAUSE I DON'T HAVE ENOUGH MONEY TO PUT OUT FOR ANYONE BUT MYSELF!!

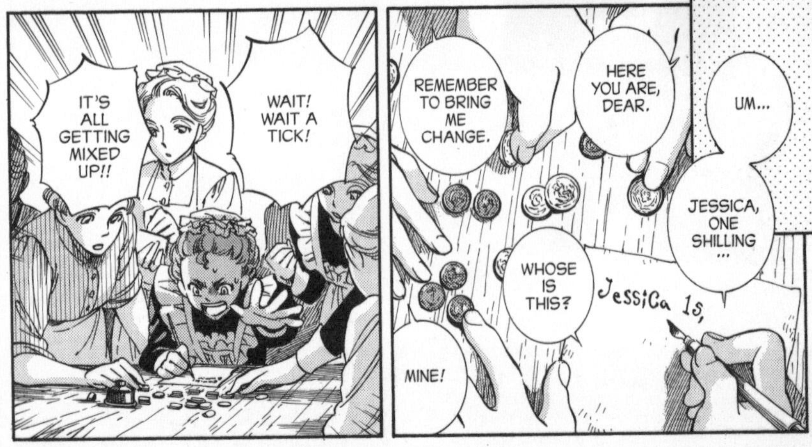
UM...
JESSICA, ONE SHILLING ...
HERE YOU ARE, DEAR.
REMEMBER TO BRING ME CHANGE.
WHOSE IS THIS?
Jessica 1s,
MINE!
WAIT! WAIT A TICK!
IT'S ALL GETTING MIXED UP!!

WHO ARE YOU, SHYLOCK?
....
I don't have any money to lend...

INSTEAD OF DOING IT THAT WAY...
...WHY NOT JUST HAVE EACH PERSON WRITE THEIR NAME AND WHAT THEY WANT ON AN ENVELOPE, THEN INSERT THE PROPER AMOUNT OF MONEY?

AH.

HERE YOU ARE, LUV.
ULP...
IN THE BLINK OF AN EYE, I'VE BEEN MADE THE SHOPPING SURROGATE OF EVERY MAID IN THIS HOUSE...
THAT FITS YOU TO A TEE, DOESN'T IT?
AFTER ALL, YOU WANTED TO GO SHOPPING.

ALMA, YOU DON'T UNDER-STAND!
WHAT'S FUN IS SHOPPING FOR MYSELF!

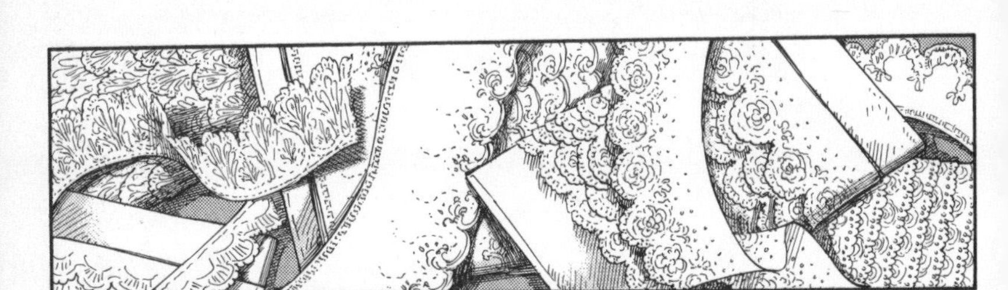

IS SHE HAVING FUN ...?

I SAY AGAIN, GIVE UP ON THAT MATERIAL.
MMM ...
YOU SIMPLY DON'T HAVE THE MONEY TO BUY IT.

THANK YOU.
PLEASE COME AGAIN.

YOU SHOULD'VE CHOSEN THAT FROM THE BEGINNING AND NOT WASTED ALL THIS TIME DILLY-DALLYING.
IT WAS TOO BEAUTIFUL TO GIVE UP THAT EASILY!

AND WHERE ARE YOU GOING TO AFFIX THAT MATERIAL?
HEH-HEH! MY UNDER-GARMENTS!

JUST MAKE SURE YOU DON'T GET CAUGHT.
THEY'VE BEEN STRICT ABOUT THAT LATELY.
DON'T WORRY, I WON'T SEW IT ONTO MY DAILIES.

AH! POLLY!
THE "ORDER" FROM THE OTHERS!

WE'D BETTER TAKE CARE OF THEM BEFORE WE FORGET.
LET'S SEE THEM.
OH, THAT'S RIGHT!

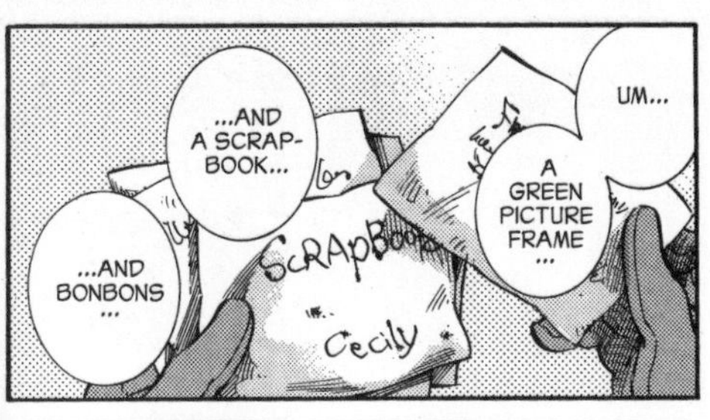
UM...
A GREEN PICTURE FRAME...
...AND A SCRAPBOOK...
...AND BONBONS...
Cecily

...AND THIS...
QUITE A FEW...

I SHOULD HAVE BROUGHT A BIGGER BAG.
NO WORRIES ON THAT ACCOUNT!
I BROUGHT ONE!

TA-DAA!!
FLAP

I REMEMBER THAT BAG...
YOU'RE GOING TO WALK AROUND WITH THAT SLUNG OVER YOUR SHOULDER?

WELL, I MADE IT MYSELF! IT'D BE A WASTE NOT TO USE IT!
I DON'T EVEN WANT TO WALK NEXT TO IT...

COME ON, ALMA!
LET'S GET THIS OVER WITH!

FENV

ISN'T THERE A GAME THAT GOES LIKE THIS?
EH?

FRY'S CHOCOLATE
CADBURYS CHOCOLATE

...BOUGHT THIS...
BOUGHT THAT...
...AND THAT...

WE'RE FINISHED FILLING EVERYONE'S ORDERS !!
NOW I CAN SHOP FOR MYSELF !!
CALM DOWN A TAD.

IS THERE SOMETHING YOU WANT TO GET, ALMA?
MMM...NOT ESPECIALLY.
WHEREVER YOU'D LIKE TO GO IS FINE.
THEN LET'S WALK THIS WAY AND SEE WHAT WE COME ACROSS!

THERE ARE MORE STORES HERE THAN I IMAGINED.
THIS IS THE BIGGEST SHOPPING DISTRICT IN THE AREA!
COME TO THINK OF IT, WHAT DO YOU USUALLY DO ON YOUR DAY OFF, ALMA?
OH, I GO TO THE RIVER, FOR EXAMPLE ...
...AND JUST STROLL AROUND ...
EH?
YOU NEED TO SHOP MORE!
IT'S FUN!

AH! ALMA, LOOK AT THAT!

HUH! THIS YEAR'S DESIGN!
BUT BLIMEY! LOOK AT THE PRICE!
New Design
25s.

I LOVE HATS...
WISH I COULD HAVE A NEW ONE...
AND WHERE WOULD YOU WEAR A HAT LIKE THAT?

MM?

HEH-HEH!

AH! FLOWERS!

THEY'RE GORGEOUS!
THANK YOU!

4 FOR 1/2d.
AH! AND CHEAP!
DAHLIAS ARE IN BLOOM ALREADY...

IT WOULD BE NICE TO BRIGHTEN UP MY ROOM WITH THEM.
ARE YOU GOING TO BUY SOME?

MMM...
NO!
NO FLOWERS OR SWEETS TODAY!!

WHAT ARE YOUR GUIDE-LINES?
I'M NOT BUYING ANYTHING THAT WILL DISAPPEAR SHORTLY AFTER I PURCHASE IT!
I'M SORRY, BUT NEXT TIME!

HELLO...
OH, GOOD AFTER-NOON.

HEH-HEH! I'M BACK AGAIN!
I JUST LOVE YOUR SHOP.

ALMA!
OVER HERE!

SCRAPS OF CLOTH?
THESE ARE ALWAYS CHEAP.
PERFECT IF YOU'RE GOING TO MAKE SOMETHING SMALL.

LIKE THAT PINCUSHION, SAY...
OH? SO THIS IS WHERE YOU BOUGHT THE MATERIAL TO MAKE THAT.

ACTUALLY, I'D LIKE TO MAKE CLOTHING AS WELL...
...BUT THAT COSTS MORE MONEY.

WHY, YOU CAN GET CLOTH FOR CLOTHES AT THE HOUSE FOR NO CHARGE.
WHAT, THAT PLAIN MATERIAL ?!

CLOTHING
...

HMM...

EH? YOU DIDN'T BUY WHAT YOU WERE LOOKING AT?
MMM... MAYBE ANOTHER TIME...

POLLY, WAIT A MOMENT.

WHAT? BOOKS?
MM.

I'M TIRED OF THE ONES AT THE MANSION.

AND IF IT'S A BOOK THAT EVERYONE COULD READ, MRS. BEEK MIGHT EVEN REIMBURSE ME FOR IT.
I SEE!

ARE THESE ALL THREE PENCE?
PER 3d.
OF COURSE, I COULD ALWAYS JUST BUY A BOOK FOR MYSELF.

IT WOULD HAVE TO BE A BOOK THAT EVERYONE WOULD READ.
WE SHOULD GET A BOOK WITH LOTS OF ILLUSTRA-TIONS.
SOME-THING INTEREST-ING.

AT THAT MOMENT, THE QUEEN'S FACE LIT UP WITH ASTONISHMENT AND EXPECTATION ...
...AND AS SHE CLASPED THE HAND OF HER BELOVED PRINCE, SHE SAID...

AH!
HOW ABOUT THIS ONE?!

THIS!! LET'S GET THIS!
THERE ARE THREE VOLUMES! A REAL VALUE!
MRS. BEEK WOULD NEVER PUT OUT MONEY FOR A THREE-VOLUME SERIES.

"YOUR WORDS MAKE ME GLOW LIKE A PEARL FROM WITHIN."
"OH, LOVELY LADY! MORE BEAUTIFUL THAN ANY CORAL FORMATION!"

AH! WHAT ABOUT MAGAZINES ?!
THEY'VE GOT STORIES PUBLISHED IN THEM!

IF YOU WANT TO READ IT SO BADLY, BUY IT YOURSELF.
EH? IN THAT CASE, NO THANK YOU.

THANK YOU...

WHAT DID YOU BUY?
OH, A TRAVEL GUIDE, A BOOK ON GARDENING ...
HUH...

WHO ARE YOU GOING TO SEND THEM TO?
MY FAMILY, MY FRIENDS IN THE COUNTRY ...

I'LL TAKE THESE!
THANK YOU.

AH... I HOPE I HAVE ENOUGH.
LET'S SEE, TRAIN FARE HOME ...

DID YOU GO THROUGH YOUR ALLOWANCE ALREADY ?
ULP ...

I...
I'M FINE!
I KEEP TRAIN FARE SEPARATE!
HERE'S YOUR CHANGE.

ARE YOU CONTENT NOW?
YES!

!
MARIA ...!

I'M SORRY, ALMA ...
...FOR DRAGGING YOU AROUND ALL DAY.
NO APOLOGY IS NECES-SARY.

IF I HAD SPENT MY DAY OFF AT THE MANSION, I'M SURE SOMEONE WOULD HAVE PUT ME TO WORK.

BESIDES I HAVE NO FAMILY OVER HERE.

....

DO YOU FEEL LIKE GOING BACK HOME TO GERMANY ?

WELL...
SOME-TIMES.

HUFF
HUFF
HUFF
HUFF

OH, LOOK AT YOU!
WHERE DID YOU COME FROM?
IS THE DOG YOURS?
NO, HE'S NOT MINE...
...BUT HE HANGS AROUND HERE BECAUSE THE CUSTOMERS ALWAYS GIVE HIM FOOD.
TOO BAD.
ALL I HAVE IS TEA!
HUFF HUFF
AHAHA! FRIENDLY MUTT, AREN'T YOU?

MM?
OH!
WHAT ABOUT MINE?
DID YOU PICK UP WHAT I ASKED FOR?!
POLLY! ALMA!
YES, WE DID.
AH! ABOUT TIME!
WE'RE BACK!
PUNCH

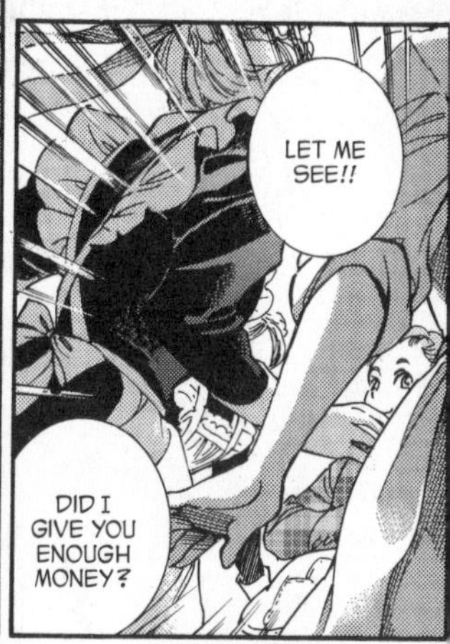
LET ME SEE!!
DID I GIVE YOU ENOUGH MONEY?

ALL RIGHT, ALL RIGHT.
DON'T ALL RUSH ME AT ONCE.

MMM...
WHICH SHALL I TAKE OUT FIRST...?
EXCUSE ME, POLLY...

LISTEN.
WE'VE BEEN WORKING ALL DAY TODAY. WE'RE EXHAUSTED...
...AND IN NO MOOD TO PRETEND THAT IT'S CHRISTMAS!
SO QUIT STALLING AND EMPTY OUT YOUR BAG.

ALL RIGHT.
IF YOU INSIST.

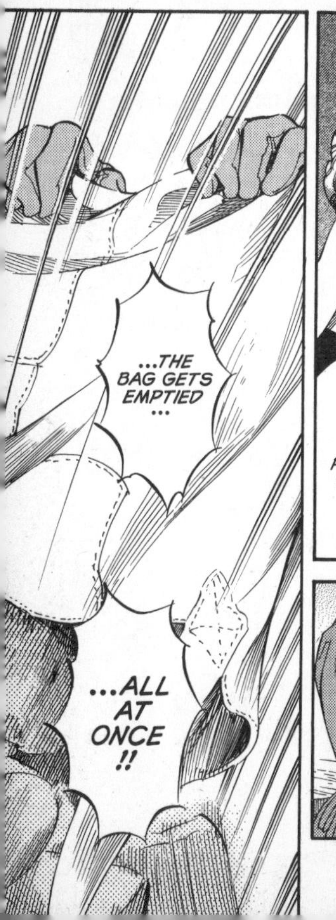
...THE BAG GETS EMPTIED...
...ALL AT ONCE!!

OHHH!!
HIGNETTS GOOD AS GOLD CIGARETTES
CHOCOL
DES CARA
HARROGATE TOFFEE
CADBURY'S CHOCOLATES
SEED
HARMSWOTH MAGAZINE
SCRAPB

CROWN
HAIR PINS
3d.
ONE HUNDRED
Tablet

CRIKEY! WHOSE ARE THESE?
HOORAY! THIS BRAND OF TOFFEES IS DELICIOUS!
AHHH, I SHOULD'VE ASKED FOR THAT!
GIVE ME ONE LATER ON!
HERE'S YOUR CHANGE.
HERE'S YOURS.
THANK YOU, POLLY!
THANK YOU TOO, ALMA.

OI, THIS IS WRONG!
I TOLD YOU PLAYERS!
ALL CIGARETTES ARE THE SAME AREN'T THEY?
I'M COLLECTING *CARDS!*

WHAT DID YOU BUY, POLLY?
HEH-HEH! WANNA SEE?
FIRST, I BOUGHT ...
THOMAS, BUY SOME CIGS FROM ME?
SIX PENSE.
THREE PENSE.
FOUR PENSE, TWO FARTHINGS....

ADELE ...
HERE.

I BOUGHT A FEW BOOKS THAT I THOUGHT EVERYONE COULD READ...
WOULD YOU PASS THEM ON TO MRS. BEEK?
CERTAINLY.

WHAT ABOUT MONEY ?
I'D BE PLEASED IF SHE REIMBURSED ME FOR THE BOOKS.

......
WHAT DID YOU SEE TODAY?

VARIOUS THINGS.
I WENT WITH POLLY HERE AND THERE.

I'M COMING TO THINK THAT IT IS FUN ONCE IN A WHILE TO GO SHOPPING WITHOUT ANY PARTICULAR PURPOSE IN MIND.
ALMA ...
DON'T LET THAT GIRL TEMPT YOU INTO THE HABIT OF SPENDING MONEY WASTEFULLY.

DON'T WORRY.
I WON'T BE GOING BACK TO TOWN FOR SOME TIME.

BUT NOW I UNDERSTAND HOW POLLY FEELS.
HOW EVEN IF YOU DON'T SPECIFICALLY WANT AN ITEM, SEEING IT BEFORE YOUR EYES MAKES YOU CRAVE IT.

IT WAS TEMPTING.
IF ONLY SHE WOULD REALIZE THAT AS WELL.

BY THE WAY, I SPOTTED MARIA IN TOWN.
SHE WAS WITH SOMEONE.

I WONDER IF SHE'S EMBARKED UPON ANOTHER AFFAIR.
......

SHOPPING IS MORE WHOLESOME THAN WHAT SHE'S UP TO, AT LEAST.
... PERHAPS YOU'RE RIGHT.

CHAPTER 11:
THREE SINGERS
(part one)

AAA
WAA
GIOACCHINO ROSSINI
IL BIRBIRE DI
SIVIGLIA
COVENT GARDEN
THEATRE
LONDON
AAAAA
AAA
AAA
WAA
BRAVO, FIGARO !!
BRAVO, ROSINA!!
BRAVO, ALMAVIVA !!
AA

CHAPTER 11: THREE SINGERS (part one)
BRAVO!!
BRAVO!!

THANK YOU!
GREAT JOB!
YOU WERE BRILLIANT TONIGHT!
THANK YOU!

YOU TOO, COUNT!!
CALL ME BY MY NAME, GEORGE!

YOU WERE MAGNIFICENT, ROSINA!!
DON'T CALL ME BY MY CHARACTER'S NAME, GEORGE!!

HE'S INCORRIGIBLE...
YOU DID DO A WONDERFUL JOB, ALAN.
NOT HALF AS WELL AS YOU, LOUISE.
AND YOU WERE EXCELLENT AS WELL, DR. BARTOLO!!
I'VE TOLD YOU MANY TIMES NOT TO CALL ME BY MY CHARACTER'S NAME.

DON'T SELL YOUR-SELF SHORT.
EVERY-THING WENT WELL TONIGHT, DIDN'T IT?
YES, SOME-HOW OR OTHER.
I CAN BREATHE A SIGH OF RELIEF.
ALL OF YOU ...
TONIGHT WAS A BRAVURA PERFORM-ANCE!
THANK YOU, SIR.
O'CONNOR ...
YOU, TOO.
THANK YOU.

GEORGE!! LOUISE!! ALAN!!

ALAN, YOU WERE FANTASTIC.
NOW YOU LOOK LIKE YOU'RE AT HOME ON THE STAGE!
SEE?!
MM?
OH, THAT'S RIGHT.
GEORGE !!
ONE MORE CURTAIN CALL!
GO!
YES, SIR!

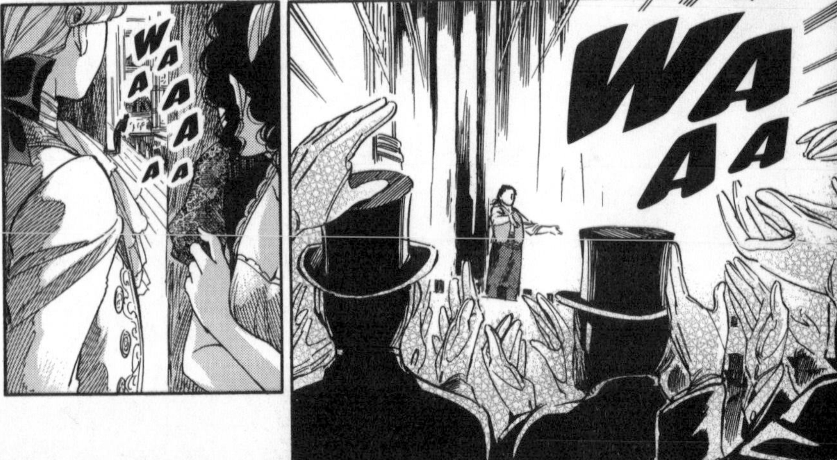
WA AA
WAAAAAAA

GEORGE IS AMAZING, ISN'T HE?
THAT ROLE IS PERFECT FOR HIM.
SO MUCH THAT IT SEEMS ODD HE HASN'T PLAYED IT BEFORE NOW.

OI, ALAN! DID YOU SEE THAT?!
SOMEONE IN THE FIRST ROW FAINTED!
I CAN'T BELIEVE THE AUDIENCE IS STANDING UP FOR YOU.

MR. O'CONNOR!
YES?

LOOK AT THIS, YOUNGSTERS.
WE'VE BEEN REVIEWED.

SO SOON?!
I WONDER IF THERE'S ANYTHING WRITTEN ABOUT ME...

UM...
LET'S SEE...

"ALTHOUGH HE DOESN'T GO BEYOND THE PRE-EXISTING IMAGE OF FIGARO...
...THE ACTOR POSSESSES A HIGH LEVEL OF ARTISTRY THAT..."
BILGE WATER! IF YOU'RE GOING TO PRAISE ME, PRAISE ME!

OH!
AH!

ALAN!
YOU'RE IN HERE, TOO!!
EH?!

ALAN BURGESS, WHO PORTRAYS COUNT ALMAVIVA, TURNED IN A GOOD PERFORMANCE, TOO.

...JUST ONE LINE?!
WHAT?! BE HAPPY!!
YOU SAID IT WAS YOUR DREAM TO GET YOUR NAME IN PRINT, REMEMBER?!

MY MENTION IS LITTLE MORE THAN A POST-SCRIPT.
AND ABOVE MY NAME, BOTH OF YOU GET TWO INCHES WORTH OF SPACE.
NOT AT ALL, MY BOY!
FOR A FIRST-TIME SOLOIST TO GET EVEN THIS MUCH SPACE IS A BIG DEAL.

AND THIS CRITIC IS KNOWN FOR SCATHING REVIEWS.
LONG AGO, HE BROUGHT THIS OLD HAM TO TEARS ON SEVERAL OCCASIONS.

THERE, YOU SEE?!
SLAP

ALAN!
OI! ALAN!
A MOMENT OF YOUR TIME!

YES?
DUCHESS BROGH IS CALLING FOR YOU.

I CAN'T STAND THAT WOMAN...
BE THAT AS IT MAY, HER FAMILY HAS BEEN A MAJOR INVESTOR IN THIS THEATRE FOR GENERATIONS.
YOU CANNOT REFUSE.

ACK!
LAST TIME, SHE MADE ME ACCOMPANY HER TO SOME FOOLISH PARTY...
I DON'T CARE, JUST GO!
LEAVE HER IN A GOOD MOOD!
FOR THE THEATRE'S SAKE!
...YES, SIR.

WHAT I DO FOR MY ART...
I'M TAKING ONE OF THESE.

MADAM BROGH.

WELL, ALAN.
YOUR ARIA WAS LOVELY.
YOU HONOR ME, MADAM.
YOU SHOULD HAVE BEEN IN THE BOX SEATS.
THAT'S ALL RIGHT, ALAN. I ENJOY VIEWING THE OPERA SURROUNDED BY FELLOW PATRONS.

I HAD NO IDEA YOU WERE COMING TONIGHT, MADAM...
...BUT I'M LUCKY THAT NO ONE TOLD ME.

I'M SURE IF I HAD KNOWN, I WOULDN'T HAVE BEEN ABLE TO SING THE ARIA AS I DID, OUT OF SHEER NERVOUSNESS.
I'M NATURALLY TIMID, YOU SEE.
HO-HOHO! OH, I DON'T BELIEVE THAT!
HO-HOHOHO-HO!

......
INCREDIBLE...

I DO FEEL A LITTLE SORRY FOR HIM, THOUGH...

......
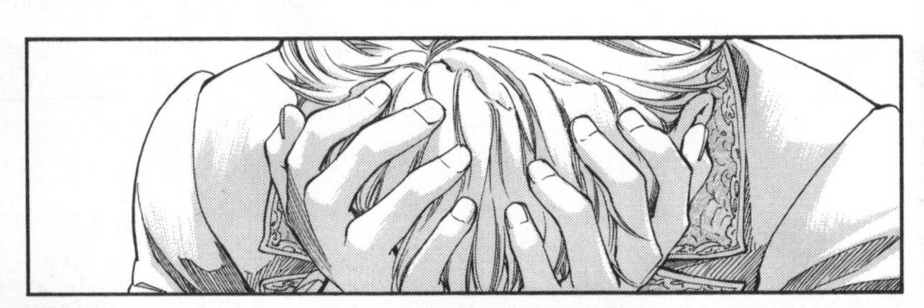

YOU GOT BAMBOOZLED INTO AGREEING TO SING AT A DINNER PARTY?!
WHAT THE DEVIL ARE YOU DOING, MAN?!
I JUST... SHE CAUGHT ME OFF GUARD ...

THE TRUTH IS, I'M NOT GOOD WITH CROWDS.
NOW, SEE HERE ...!

YOU ARE A FAVORITE OF OPERA-GOING MARRIED WOMEN ALL OVER LONDON.
I DON'T TO WANT TO HEAR THAT!

IT'S A MISFORTUNE, ALAN...
...BUT BEING FAVORED IS A DOUBLE-EDGED SWORD.

ALL OF US BOW TO OUR PATRONS TO A GREATER OR LESSER EXTENT.
IT'S NOTHING TO BE ASHAMED OF.

I'M WELL AWARE THAT MY MODICUM OF POPULARITY STEMS FROM MY LOOKS, NOT FROM MY SINGING.
ALAN, DON'T TALK LIKE THAT.

WHAT ABOUT THAT OTHER WOMAN WHO WAS HERE LAST TIME?
OR THAT COUNTESS?

BUT...
...SHE'S NOT MY PATRON.
NO?

...THANK YOU, LOUISE.

TO BE HONEST ...

...IF I CHOSE ONE, I WOULD BE AFRAID OF THE REST.
MANY MEN WOULD LOVE TO HAVE YOUR PROB-LEMS.

ME, I HAVEN'T HAD A SINGLE PATRON! I HAD TO SCRAPE BY FOR YEARS!
THAT'S *YOU*, GEORGE ...
THAT'S GEORGE ...

DID YOU HAVE A PATRON, LOUISE?
WELL ...
THERE WERE CERTAIN PEOPLE WHO HELPED TAKE CARE OF ME WHEN I WAS JUST STARTING OUT...

TOOK CARE OF YOU...

DON'T TELL ME YOU...

YOU KNOW ABOUT THOSE KINDS OF MEN!
THEY "GROOM" A GIRL WHO CATCHES THEIR EYE, RAISE HER TO A CERTAIN LEVEL OF FAME AND THEN IT'S OVER ONCE THEY TIRE OF HER!

DON'T EVEN JEST ABOUT THINGS LIKE THAT!!
OWWW !!

BE THAT AS IT MAY, IT'S HARD HAVING TO CONSTANTLY FLATTER PEOPLE TO WIN THEIR FAVOR.

....

OF COURSE IF THE WOMAN'S A POPULAR SINGER, THE STORY'S DIFFERENT. THEN THEY WISH TO BECOME HER LOVER...
WHEREAS THEY CONSIDER A NOVICE CHANTEUSE BENEATH THEM.

I WANT TO QUICKLY GET TO THE LEVEL THE TWO OF YOU ARE AT, WHERE I CAN RELY ON MY VOICE ALONE.
ALAN...
OI, ALAN!

YOU AND I GREW UP TOGETHER. EVER SINCE WE WERE URCHINS, OUR HEARTS WERE SET ON GETTING HERE! THAT'S THE MAN I WANT TO PERFORM WITH.
AREN'T YOU THRILLED TO BE HERE?
I KNOW I AM!

YOU HEARD THE CROWD OUT THERE.
THEY WERE YELLING YOUR NAME, TOO.
SINGING ISN'T ABOUT TRYING TO CATCH UP TO SOMEONE.

...YOU'RE RIGHT.
SORRY.

DON'T WORRY, I DON'T ACT AS FAWNING AS I MADE IT SOUND.
...I KNOW.

SEE YOU TOMORROW.
DON'T BE LATE, GEORGE.
I WON'T.

GOOD MORNING, ALAN.
GOOD MORNING.

LOUISE?
ULP!
ALAN?!

WHAT ARE YOU DOING?
DID YOU DROP AN EARRING OR ...?
I'M LOOKING FOR A CAT.
HAVE YOU SEEN IT?

A CAT?

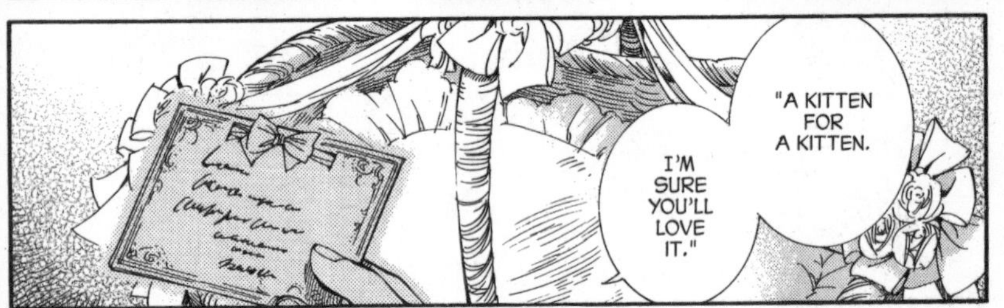
"A KITTEN FOR A KITTEN.
I'M SURE YOU'LL LOVE IT."

... CERTAINLY IS CORNY.
THE POINT IS, SOME FOOLISH SOD SENT ME A LIVE CAT!!

HALLO, MISS LOUISE!
ANOTHER LOAD HAS ARRIVED TODAY!
I'M JUST GOING TO SET THEM DOWN HERE...
THUD
THUD

COMING THROUGH! COMING THROUGH!
CLOMP
CLOMP
CLOMP

WHEN WAS IT DELIVERED?
I BELIEVE ABOUT TWO HOURS AGO.

THIS IS A DANGEROUS AREA, WITH PEOPLE ALWAYS GOING BACK AND FORTH...
WHAT IF IT GETS STEPPED ON?!

DID YOU LEAVE THE DOOR OPEN THIS WHOLE TIME?
I CAN'T HELP IT...

MISS LOUISE...

AH, IN THERE, PLEASE.
WHEREVER THERE'S SPACE.

THAT DOOR WON'T STAY SHUT FOR MORE THAN A FEW SECONDS, WILL IT?
......

ALAN, WILL YOU SEARCH WITH ME?!
ALL RIGHT, ALL RIGHT.
I HAVE NO DESIRE TO STUMBLE INTO A DEAD ANIMAL LATE AT NIGHT EITHER.

THIS IS WHAT YOU WERE TALKING ABOUT AGAIN, THE "DOUBLE-EDGED SWORD" OF BEING POPULAR, EH?
......

HERE, KITTY-KITTY!
COME OUT, COME OUT...
...WHER-EVER YOU ARE!

I WONDER IF IT LISTENS TO SUCH ENTREAT-IES.
THIS IS WHAT YOU SAY WHEN YOU LOOK FOR AN ANIMAL!!

HAVEN'T SEEN IT.

NO, I HAVEN'T SEEN ANY CAT AROUND HERE.

A KITTEN?
OH, ALAN, YOU'RE A NAUGHTY ONE!

WHERE DOES THIS "KITTEN" HAIL FROM?
IS SHE THE KIND THAT SITS ON YOUR LAP AND PESTERS YOU TO BUY HER THINGS?
NO, NO, NO!!
THE REAL THING!
WITH FOUR LEGS AND A TAIL!!

OH, ALAN!
THANK YOU FOR THE CHAIR!

ALAN! THOSE CLOTHES YOU GAVE ME LAST TIME REALLY CAME IN HANDY!
THEY FIT MY HUSBAND PERFECT-LY!

ALAN!
IF YOU EVER GET ANOTHER FINE PAINTING, SEND IT MY WAY AGAIN!

YOU'RE VERY CHARITABLE.
ONLY WITH THE THINGS THE CONTINGENT OF WIVES GIVE ME.

YOU GIVE PRESENTS AWAY?!
I LIVE IN A BOARDING HOUSE!!
I DON'T HAVE ROOM FOR ALL THE GIFTS I'M GIVEN!!

SAY...
HOW FAR DOES A CAT ROAM, ANYHOW?
IT DEPENDS ON THE SIZE...
...BUT A FEW HOURS HAVE PASSED...

LOUISE...
LET'S GIVE UP ON THIS.
IF WE HAVEN'T FOUND THE BEAST BY NOW, WE'RE NOT GOING TO.
BUT...!

IT'S NOT YOUR RESPONSIBILITY.
ALAN!

EVEN IF SOMETHING DID HAPPEN TO IT, IT MUST'VE HAPPENED SOMEWHERE WE'RE NOT GOING TO SEE, SO IT'S ALL RIGHT.
ALAN!!

......
I'M SORRY.

YOUR ADMIRER IS TO BLAME FOR THIS.
YOU NEVER ASKED FOR A PET.

MEOW...

THERE IT IS...

A WHITE CAT ON A WHITE BLANKET.
THANK HEAVENS...
NO WONDER WE DIDN'T FIND IT. IT MUST'VE BEEN SLEEPING.
Blended right in...

WELL?

I DON'T KNOW. I'M HARDLY EVER AT HOME...
AND *MY* LANDLADY HATES CATS...

DO YOU HAVE A MAID?
YES, BUT...

...SHE'S ALLERGIC, APPARENT-LY.
AH...

A CAT?

I'LL TAKE IT OFF YOUR HANDS.
GEORGE, DON'T HANDLE IT SO ROUGHLY...!

NOT FOR MYSELF ...
...BUT RECENTLY, MY NIECE HAS SAID SHE WANTS A KITTEN...
...SO I'LL GIVE IT TO HER.

REALLY ?!
THANK YOU, GEORGE !!

WHY DID LOUISE BEHAVE LIKE THAT OVER A CAT?

YOU DON'T KNOW?
EH?

BEFORE LOUISE BECAME SO BUSY, I TAKE IT SHE HAD MANY CATS.
SHE SAID ONE WAS RUN OVER IN THE STREET BY A CARRIAGE.

PROBABLY HAD THAT ONE ON HER MIND WHILE HUNTING THIS LITTLE FELLA DOWN.
....

A CAT ...

ARE YOU ALONE, MISTER?

IT'S A COLD NIGHT.

BUT IF YOU'RE WITH SOMEONE, IT CAN BE WARM.

HAVE YOU HAD DINNER?
EH?

THIS IS THE FIRST TIME A CUSTOMER HAS EVER TREATED ME TO A MEAL.
JUST FILL UP.

ARE YOU SURE IT'S OKAY?
YES. YOU'RE HUNGRY, AREN'T YOU?

YOU'RE A GOOD MAN, SIR.

WHY DID YOU COME UP TO ME?
DID I LOOK SO BORED?
LONELY MORE THAN BORED.
I THOUGHT MAYBE I HAD A CHANCE.

......

OH, I DON'T MEAN FOR YOU TO GET GLOOMY!
I ONLY SAID YOU LOOKED LONELY.

CREAK

FWAP

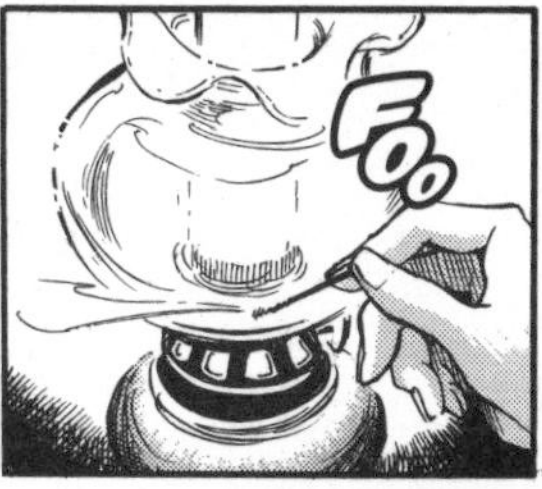
FOO

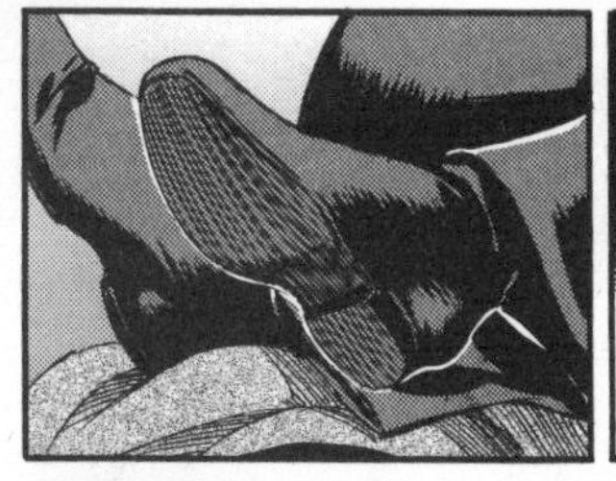

L'amoroso sincero
(SINCERE AND BELOVED...)
Lindoro
(...LINDORO...)

Non può darvi,
(...CANNOT OFFER YOU...)
mia cara, un tesoro
(...A THING.)
Io ——...
(I...)

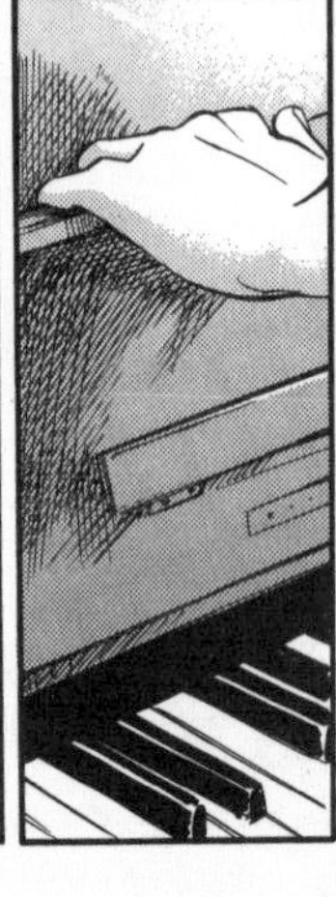

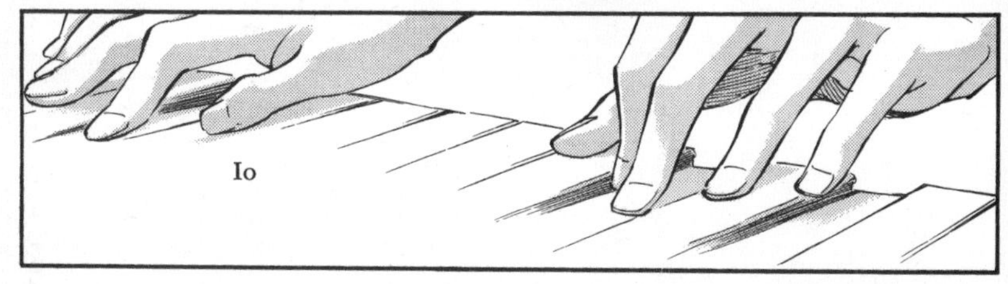
Io

Io ricco non sono,
(...I AM NOT RICH...)
Ma un core vi dono,
(...BUT MY HEART, I GIVE...)

Un'anima amante
(...A LOVE THAT IS CONSTANT...)
Che fida e constante
(...AND TRUE)
REALLY?! YOU'RE A SINGER?!

I WORK AT THE THEATER ONCE IN A WHILE.
MAYBE YOU'VE SEEN ME BEFORE?
I DON'T BELIEVE SO, NO.

DO YOU HAVE A SWEET-HEART?

A SWEET-HEART? NO.

SOMEONE THAT YOU'RE SWEET ON, THEN!

....
I CAN'T DENY IT.

LUCKY GIRL!
I WISH SOMEONE HAD FEELINGS LIKE THAT FOR ME!
THEN WE COULD GET MARRIED!

HAVE YOU TOLD HER YOU LOVE HER?
NO, NOT YET.

AREN'T YOU GOING TO TELL HER?
I'VE BEEN MEANING TO, BUT...

WHEN?

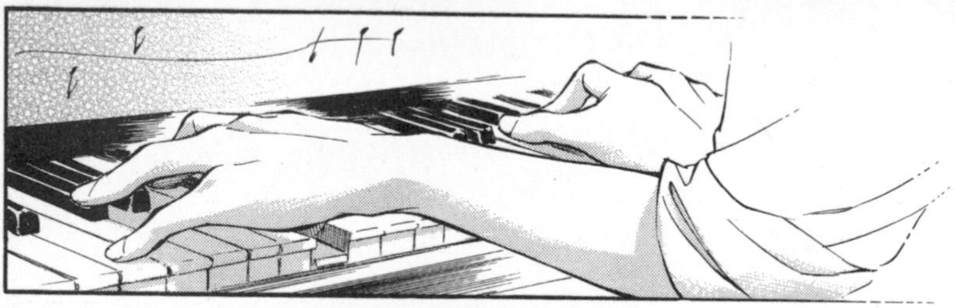

MR. BURGESS!

MR. BURGESS!
IT'S LATE. WOULD YOU MIND PUTTING OFF YOUR PRACTICING UNTIL TOMORROW?

CERTAINLY. I BEG YOUR PARDON.

THUMP

AS I RECALL, LOUISE MILLER, WHO PLAYS ROSINA ...
...ALSO APPEARED IN THIS THEATER'S LAST PRODUCTION OF "OTHELLO".
AH!
I SAW IT, TOO. THE MUSIC WAS LOVELY.

ALAN BURGESS PLAYS COUNT ALMAVIVA ...
I HAVEN'T HEARD OF HIM.
PER-HAPS HE'S A NEW-COMER.

THE OVERTURE IS DONE!
IS EVERYTHING READY?
EVERYONE'S HERE?
DON'T STUMBLE WHILE WALKING OUT ON STAGE.

ARE YOU NERVOUS... ...ALAN?

LOUISE...
EVERY PERFORMANCE 'TIL NOW HAS GONE SMOOTHLY...
...AND SO WILL THIS EVENING'S.

THAT'S WHAT I'M TRYING TO CONVINCE MYSELF.

IT'LL BE ALL RIGHT.
JUST ACT NORMALLY.

ACT NORMALLY.

YOU PROBABLY DON'T GET BUTTERFLIES IN THE STOMACH, DO YOU, LOUISE?

OH, I DO.
ALWAYS.
ENOUGH TO MAKE ME WANT TO FLEE THE THEATRE, TO BE HONEST.

"AREN'T YOU GOING TO TELL HER?"

IT'S STARTING.

"WHEN?"

"I'VE BEEN MEANING TO, BUT ..."

"AFTER OUR NEXT PERFORMANCE."

CHAPTER 12:
THREE SINGERS
(part two)

London

......

CHAPTER 12: THREE SINGERS (part two)
AH!!

AMELIA!!
WHAT DID YOU DO?!

LETTERS THAT YOU HESITATE BEFORE OPENING...
...SHOULDN'T BE READ, MISS LOUISE.

IT COULD'VE BEEN IMPORTANT...!!
REALLY?

......
NO, NOT REALLY.
ALL RIGHT.

HOW DID YOU KNOW?

I KNOW YOU WELL ENOUGH...
...TO DISCERN HOW YOU FEEL BY LOOKING AT THE EXPRESSION ON YOUR FACE.

TO TELL YOU THE TRUTH...
...I WAS PONDERING WHETHER TO RIP IT TO SHREDS OR BURN IT.
BURNING IT WAS THE PROPER RESPONSE.
LEAVES LESS OF A CLEAN-UP AFTER-WARDS.

SAY, AMELIA ...
ARE THESE ALL THE LETTERS?
YES. FROM THE PEOPLE THAT KNOW YOU, ANYWAY.

AND THE REST?
THERE ARE ABOUT TWO BUCKETS WORTH OF FAN MAIL.
LIGHT DAY.
INDEED.
......

......
I WANT A CAT...
I WANT ...
AMELIA, I WANT A CAT...
MISS LOUISE.

IT ISN'T AS THOUGH I DESPISE CATS.
I HAVE A CONSTITUTIONAL WEAKNESS. THERE ISN'T ANYTHING FOR IT.

AMELIA ...
SAY, "MEOW".
ARE YOU LISTENING TO ME, MISS LOUISE?

MEOW ...

MEOWW ...

YOU SOUND LIKE AN ILL-HUMORED CAT.
Like a small child's caught your tail...
I FEEL ILL-HUMORED AT THE MOMENT.

ANYWAY, YOU'RE BUSY WITH WORK RIGHT NOW.
WHY DON'T YOU RAISE A CAT WHEN YOU HAVE MORE FREE TIME?
FREE TIME ...

THAT REMINDS ME, AMELIA.
I WONDER WHAT I SHOULD DO ABOUT THAT OTHER SUBJECT ...

DON'T YOU TELL ME YOU'RE THINKING OF AGREEING JUST SO YOU CAN HAVE A CAT...?
NO, OF COURSE NOT!
THE TWO TOPICS HAVE NOTHING TO DO WITH ONE ANOTHER !!

I'M FLUMMOXED.
WELL, IT ISN'T A SUBJECT I FEEL COMFORT-ABLE WEIGHING IN ON...

AMELIA, PLEASE LET ME HEAR YOUR OPINION!
YOU'RE THE ONLY PERSON I CAN ASK ABOUT THIS!!
ALL RIGHT, ALL RIGHT. IF I MUST...

IT APPEARS TO ME...
...THAT YOU'VE ALREADY MADE YOUR DECISION...
...MISS LOUISE.

BUT YOU JUST HAVEN'T SET YOUR MIND TO IT...
...AND WANT ME TO GIVE YOU A PUSH.

That's not a very good way to look to someone for help.
I know.

ALL RIGHT, THEN.
I'VE DECIDED.

IT ISN'T AS IF I'M GIVING UP SINGING.
THERE. I'M BEING DECISIVE.

I CAN'T VERY WELL WAVER FOREVER.

YOUR VOICE TEACHER SHALL BE HERE SHORTLY.
EH?!
IT'S THAT TIME ALREADY ?!

THAT'S RIGHT.
YOU CAN'T.

WELCOME, MR. MONTAGUE.
THANK YOU FOR COMING.

THANK YOU, AMELIA.
YOU'RE AS TALL AS EVER TODAY.
THANK YOU.

WELL, WELL, LOUISE.
I'M TEN MINUTES LATE, BUT IT FEELS LIKE I'M EARLY.
OH, NO, SIR ...

......

SUPERB ...

UMM ...
MR. MONTAGUE?
MM?

THERE'S SOMETHING I'D LIKE TO DISCUSS WITH YOU.

RETIRE?
YOU'RE GOING TO RETIRE?

NOT RIGHT AWAY, BUT...

DON'T YOU THINK IT'S A LITTLE EARLY IN YOUR CAREER?
YES.

BUT I'VE THOUGHT OVER ...
... VARIOUS THINGS.

AND THINGS HAVE JUST COME TOGETHER FOR ME RECENTLY ...
NOTHING ESPECIALLY WORTH MENTIONING ...

AT ANY RATE, I DON'T INTEND TO QUIT SINGING.
JUST RETIRE FROM THE THEATRE.

I WAS THINKING ABOUT CONTINUING MY CAREER BY SINGING IN SMALLER VENUES.
SMALLER VENUES?

LIKE SALONS... THERE ARE MANY PLACES THAT WELCOME CHANTEUSES.

WELL, THAT'S TRUE.

I CAN EVEN IMAGINE GOING BACK TO THE THEATRE, FROM TIME TO TIME...
...BUT WITH A LIMITED NUMBER OF PERFORMANCES.

I SUPPOSE I WANT TO FOCUS MORE ON THE SINGING ASPECT OF MY CAREER...

....

HM. WELL...
...IF THAT'S YOUR DECISION...

...I WISH YOU GOOD LUCK WITH IT.
THANK YOU.

COME TO THINK OF IT, AMELIA ...
YOU HAVEN'T SEEN ANY OF LOUISE'S PERFORMANCES YET, HAVE YOU?

....

YOU OUGHT TO GO WHILE YOU STILL HAVE THE CHANCE.
UM, MR. MONTAGUE ...

AMELIA HAS COME TO SEE ME PERFORM BEFORE ...
ONCE.

IT WAS MY FIRST PERFORMANCE ON STAGE, AS A MATTER OF FACT, AND SHE WAS THERE TO COMMEMORATE THE OCCASION...

....

... AND?

I DON'T NEED TO GO BACK TO AN UNCIVILIZED PLACE LIKE THAT, THANK YOU VERY MUCH.

SHE WAS SITTING IN THE GALLERY AND THERE SEEM TO HAVE BEEN MANY FRANK AUDIENCE MEMBERS UP THERE...

IS THAT SOPRANO A NEWCOMER? SHE'S AWFUL.

A DISTURBANCE ENSUED ...

WHAP
ACK!

KEEP YOUR OPINIONS TO YOURSELF !!
WHAT THE DEVIL WAS THAT FOR?!

SO THAT WAS BECAUSE OF YOU TWO, EH?
AHHH, YES. I REMEMBER SOMETHING OF THE SORT.

WHEN SOMEONE'S DOING THE BEST JOB THAT SHE CAN, HOW COULD ANYONE THINK TO HECKLE HER?!

I HAVE TO ADMIT, I WAS PRETTY BAD...
Back then
MMM ...

IN THAT CASE, YOU SHOULD TRY COMING BACK ONE MORE TIME.
RIGHT NOW, LOUISE ENJOYS HIGH PRAISE FROM ALL CORNERS.

DON'T YOU WANT TO SEE HOW THE RESULTS OF ALL HER PRACTICING HAVE PAID OFF?

CAN I HAVE A LITTLE TIME TO THINK ABOUT IT?
AMELIA ?!
Ha ha ha
OF COURSE, OF COURSE!

WELL, I SHOULD GET GOING.
THANK YOU FOR THE TEA.

NO MATTER HOW OFTEN I COME HERE, THERE'S ALWAYS AN ABUNDANCE OF BEAUTIFUL FLOWERS.

THEY KEEP THE AIR IN HERE FROM GETTING DRY.

WHERE ARE YOU OFF TO?
I HAVE A LESSON WITH ALAN AT MY HOME.

COMPARED TO YOU AND GEORGE, HE GOT A LATE START...
...BUT ALAN'S MAKING CONSIDERABLE PROGRESS.

ALTHOUGH I'M SURE YOU'VE NOTICED, JUST PERFORMING WITH HIM.
YES.

TAKE CARE.

ALAN.

AH, EXCUSE ME.
I DON'T MIND.

YOU'VE GOT A VERY NICE PIANO.
THE ONE I HAVE IS SHOT.

I HOPE TO BE ABLE TO BUY SOMETHING AS FINE AS THIS ONE OF THESE DAYS.
OH, I'M SURE YOU WILL.

HOW GO THE PERFORMANCES?
WELL, I EXPECT?

I FEEL LIKE THE DIFFERING LEVELS OF TALENT BETWEEN ME AND THOSE TWO IS ON DISPLAY FOR ALL TO SEE.
OH, DEAR.

I MAKE IT A POINT NOT TO TEACH PUPILS WHO HAVE NO PROSPECTS.
IT ONLY RESULTS IN HEARTACHE FOR THE BOTH OF US.

THIS IS NOTHING NEW TO ME...
I JUST... TO BE HONEST, I DON'T KNOW WHAT TO DO...

KEEP CHEWING ON IT.
IT'S THE PREROGATIVE OF YOUTH WHO HAVE TIME ON THEIR HANDS.

OH, YES.
THAT REMINDS ME, I JUST CAME FROM LOUISE'S HOME...

LOUISE, YOU'RE GOING TO RETIRE ?!

OH, ALAN!
GOOD MORNING, ALAN.
THAT'S RIGHT.

WHY ...?
MY CONTRACT WITH THE THEATRE IS UP THIS YEAR...
...AND IT JUST SEEMED LIKE PERFECT TIMING ...

BUT WHAT A WASTE.
I'M SURE YOU HAVEN'T REACHED THE HEIGHT OF YOUR POPULARITY... AND YOUR VOICE...
IT WOULD BE SAD TO RETIRE WHEN EITHER OR BOTH WERE WANING.

I CAN LIVE WITH PEOPLE THINKING MY RETIREMENT IS A WASTE OF TALENT.

THEN WHAT WILL YOU DO? MOVE TO THE COUNTRY-SIDE?
I'D HARDLY EVER BE ABLE TO SEE YOU.
OH, WE'LL BE ABLE TO SEE EACH OTHER OFTEN ENOUGH.

GEORGE'S HOUSE IS NEAR HERE, ISN'T IT?

GEORGE?
YES, WE WERE JUST TALKING ABOUT IT, BUT...

OLD CHAP, WE'RE GETTING MARRIED.
YOU AND LOUISE?
YES, THAT'S RIGHT.
...WHY?
WHY...?
SLAP
WHY, LOUISE CONFESSED THAT SHE'S OVER THE MOON FOR ME AND...
I SAID NO SUCH THING!!
WELL, IT WAS SOMETHING TO THAT EFFECT!
WHAT?! YOU WERE THE ONE WHO FIRST BROACHED THE SUBJECT OF YOUR FEELINGS TO ME!!
...I SEE.

WELL, I GUESS ...
CONGRATULATIONS.
WHAT'S THE "I GUESS" PART FOR?!
And what's with the hand ?!

NO, I MEAN... GOOD LUCK.
SHE *IS* LOUISE.
OH.
EXCUSE ME?! ALAN, WHAT'S THAT SUPPOSED TO MEAN?!

GOOD LUCK TO YOU, TOO, LOUISE.
HIS HOUSE IS BIG, BUT DIRTY.
...I KNOW.
I've seen it.

HAVE YOU TOLD EVERYONE?
WE RAN INTO MR. O'CONNOR EARLIER AND TOLD HIM...
...BUT YOU'RE THE ONLY OTHER PERSON SO FAR.

WE HAVE TO THINK ABOUT TIMING.
WE'VE JUST DECIDED TO GET MARRIED. EVERYTHING THAT FOLLOWS IS STILL UP IN THE AIR.
THINGS ARE SO HECTIC HERE...
MM, YES ...

ONCE THINGS SETTLE DOWN, COME OVER TO THE HOUSE.
IT'S BEEN TOO LONG SINCE THE THREE OF US HAD DINNER TOGETHER.

...I'D LOVE TO.

GEORGE! LOUISE!
THEY SENT ME TO CALL YOU TO REHEARS-ALS!

ON OUR WAY.

ALAN!
ONCE THESE TWO ARE DONE, YOU'RE UP!
ALL RIGHT.

OH, ALAN!
MR. O'CONNOR?
WHAT'S WRONG?
WHAT ARE YOU DOING UP HERE?
DRINKING?
I TIPPLE FROM TIME TO TIME.
AND THIS ISN'T A BAD PLACE FOR IT.

LET ME ASK YOU THE SAME QUESTION.
WHAT ARE *YOU* DOING HERE?

NOTHING ESPECIAL-LY...
JUST... SEEMED LIKE A PLACE TO GO...

MR. O'CONNOR ...
MM?

WHERE'S THAT COMING FROM?

IT'S TRUE.

I'M GLAD I GOT THE CHANCE TO PERFORM TOGETHER WITH YOU.

FROM HERE.

MY HEAD?

BOTH HE AND I...
...GREW UP LOOKING DOWN ON YOUR HEAD.

WELL, I'LL BE...
YOU BOYS TOO, EH?

WE WANTED TO HEAR YOUR PERFOR-MANCES SO BADLY...
...THAT WE OFTEN SNUCK UP HERE.

BACK THEN, THE GREAT ITALIAN SINGERS WERE THOUGHT OF AS GODS.

I DID THE SAME.
BESEECHED THE CURTAIN-PULLER AND HE LET ME UP HERE.

...YOU'RE GOD TO ME, MR. O'CONNOR.

ACTUALLY, I LONGED TO BE A BASS LIKE YOU...
...BUT I COULDN'T DO ANYTHING ABOUT THE QUALITY OF MY VOICE.
HA-HA-HA!
THERE'S NOTHING WRONG WITH BEING A TENOR.

WHY, ON STAGE, NO MATTER HOW BEAUTIFUL THE PRIMA DONNA, SHE BECOMES YOUR SWEET-HEART.
I'M ENVIOUS.

....
THAT'S ONLY ON STAGE.

HAVE YOU HEARD AS WELL?

Ha un gran
(TO BE HONEST...)
difetto addosso.
(...HE HAS ONE MAJOR PROBLEM.)
Un gran difetto...?
(A MAJOR PROBLEM...?)

YES.
THOSE TWO ARE GOING TO GET MARRIED.

Ah, grande...
(YES, INDEED...)
e innamorato morto
(YOU SEE, HE IS DYING OF LOVE.)
Si, davvero?
(OH, IS THAT SO?)

E la sua bella,
(AND TELL ME, THIS WOMAN THAT HE LOVES...)
dite, abita lontano?
(...DOES SHE LIVE FAR AWAY?)
Oh no!... cioe...
(OH, NOT AT ALL!)
Qui... due passi...
(IN FACT...SHE'S RIGHT HERE...)

Ma e bella?
(IS SHE PRETTY?)

I WONDER IF LOUISE KNOWS ...

...HOW YOU FEEL ABOUT HER.

Oh, bella assai!
(YES, VERY MUCH SO!)
Grassotta, genialotta,
(WITH A PLEASINGLY PLUMP, INTELLIGENT FACE.)
capello nero, guancia porporina...
(BLACK HAIR, CHEEKS THE COLOR OF ROSES...)

tu non m'inganni?
(YOU'RE NOT LYING TO ME NOW, ARE YOU?)
Dunque io son
(THEN I AM...)
la fortunata
(...THE FORTUNATE GIRL!)

Dunque
(THEN...)
io son
(...IT IS I...)

I DON'T THINK SHE DOES.
AND I'D LIKE TO KEEP IT THAT WAY.
....
Gia me l'ero immaginata
(I HAD THOUGHT SO ERE NOW...)
lo sapeva pria di te
(...BEFORE YOU HAD EVEN HINTED AT IT.)

YET YOU SAW THROUGH ME?
A GUT FEELING, NO MORE.
BUT I BELIEVE I'M THE ONLY ONE TO HAVE NOTICED.
I'D RESOLVED TO TELL HER HOW I FELT AFTER TONIGHT'S PERFORMANCE.
CLOSE SHAVE.
AYE, INDEED.
AND I WAS JUST AS SURPRISED TO HEAR THE NEWS AS YOU.

......

MIND IF I HAVE A PULL OF THAT?
NOT AT ALL, BUT MY GLASS IS...

Right from there is fine.
From the thermos?

I JUST DON'T KNOW...
IS THIS WHAT MY LIFE IS?
CAREFUL, SON. THAT'S BAD BOOZE.

I WANT TO LIVE... ON SINGING ALONE.

GOOD LORD.

BUT ...
... SONGS ...
...ARE SUNG BY *PEOPLE*.

MAYBE...

...THE TRUTH IS...
...I DON'T REALLY MIND SO MUCH...
...CURRYING FAVOR WITH MY PATRONS.

THERE ARE CERTAIN ASPECTS THAT I DISLIKE...
...AND I THINK IT'S ODD...

BUT IT'S GRATIFYING TO PLEASE PEOPLE.

DAMN IT. THEY LOOK SO HAPPY TOGETHER.
......
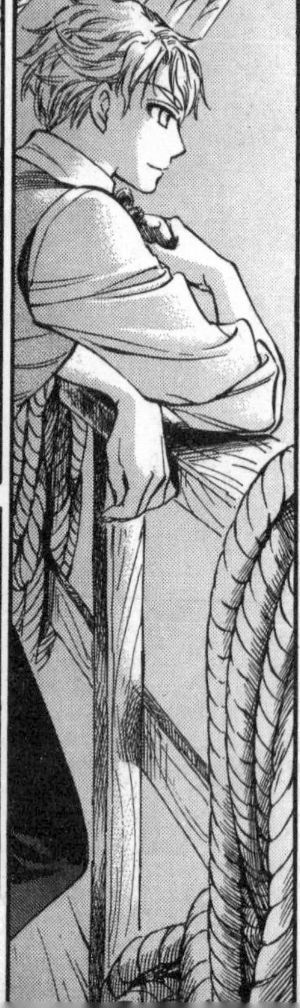

WHICH ITALIAN SINGER WAS YOUR IDOL, MR. O'CONNOR ?
MM?

OH.
THERE WERE SEVERAL.
ALL DEAD NOW, THOUGH.

WHO WAS NUMBER ONE?
NO, THEY WERE ALL MAGNIFI-CENT...
...IN THEIR OWN WAY.
I NEVER THOUGHT OF IT LIKE THAT.
PLEASE, TELL ME WHO THEY WERE.
WELL, LET ME SEE...
THE FIRST SINGER THAT I HEARD WAS...
......

?
DO YOU SMELL LIQUOR?
MUST BE YOUR IMAGINATION.

LET'S HAVE GEORGE AND ALAN RUN THROUGH IT ONCE!
THANK YOU, LOUISE!

ALL RIGHT.
ALAN! HE WANTS YOU AND GEORGE ON STAGE.

OH!
AREN'T YOU FULL OF SPIRIT?
COME ON, GEORGE!
YOU READY ?!

WHAT THE HELL ARE YOU GOING ON ABOUT?
THE POWER OF DESPAIR CAN BE A GREAT THING.
AH, GO AHEAD.
I SUP-POSE ...
BUT HAVING HIGH SPIRITS IS THE ONLY WAY I CAN GET THROUGH THIS.

DO YOU MIND IF I SIT NEXT TO YOU?

GO AHEAD.

EXCUSE ME...
CAN YOU READ?

HOW'S THE CROWD?
NOT BAD.

WE COULD USE MORE BOX SEATS...
THEY'RE PACKED IN UP AT THE TOP.

LET ME SEE...

I KNOW HIM, YOU KNOW.

A COUNT ?!

WHY, THAT'S WONDERFUL! HE MUST BE VERY IMPORTANT!

AND I'M A FRIEND OF MISS LOUISE.
MISS LOUISE ?

AMELIA, THIS IS TOO SOON !!
WAIT A TICK. NEXT TO HER...IS THAT ...?
She's here ...?

AMELIA ...!!

HERE, "ROSINA".
THE MOST IMPORTANT CHARACTER OF ALL.
REALLY? MORE IMPORTANT THAN A COUNT?

ULP... ALL OF A SUDDEN, MY BUTTER-FLIES HAVE BUTTER-FLIES...
ME TOO ...
COME ON, LET'S KNOCK 'EM DEAD!!

OI!
COME ON, BOTH OF YOU!!

AFTERWORD

SILLY AFTERWORD MANGA

WOMEN AREN'T BORN MAIDS. THEY BECOME MAIDS.
DEVOTE YOURSELVES, ROOKIES.
Yes, ma'am!
GREETINGS, EVERYONE. THANK YOU FOR BUYING EMMA VOLUME NINE.
TO COMPENSATE FOR THE ABRUPT DECLINE IN MAID MATERIAL SINCE THIS BOOK HAS BECOME FOCUSED ON TELLING "SIDE STORIES", I, AMELIA, SHALL HOST THIS AFTERWORD FOR NO PARTICULAR REASON.
......
For no particular reason?

No particular reason?
No, no, there is a reason. For example, you can do it for my sake...

ANY-WAY...
...THIS IS VOLUME NINE!!
HOW TO GET THROUGH LIFE'S STORMY SEAS...
USE A LOUD VOICE TO DISPEL AN UNCOMFORTABLE ATMOSPHERE!

....

WELL, THIS VOLUME MARKS THE SECOND ONE COMPILED OF "SIDE STORIES"...
...AND IT'S ALONG THE SAME LINES AS THE PREVIOUS VOLUME.

ALTHOUGH I RAISE AN EYEBROW AT THE INCLUSION OF THE LAST STORY, ABOUT THE SINGERS.
"SIDE STORY"? THIS HAS ABSOLUTELY NOTHING TO DO WITH ANY OF THE PREVIOUSLY ESTABLISHED CHARACTERS.

But I wanted to do that story!
I've heard that before...

...WHEN APPLYING THE SCREENTONES IS HOW TO "MAKE THE CHEST AND ARMS LOOK BEAUTIFUL" OR HOW TO "GIVE IT AN EROTIC QUALITY"... IN OTHER WORDS, I FOCUS ON THE SENSUAL ASPECTS AND IGNORE EVERYTHING ELSE...

I don't care! I like drawing sensual material!
Saying it in a cute manner doesn't excuse you.

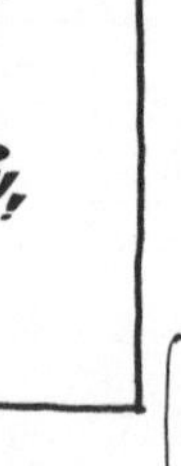

HMPH!

MY MAJOR WAS SANSKRIT LITERATURE AND HINDU PHILOSOPHY.
T.ENNIS:FOR BEGINNERS

SUBASH CHANDRA (26)

I CAME UP WITH HIS NAME, BUT DIDN'T GET A CHANCE TO USE IT IN THE STORY. AFTER GRADUATING FROM UNIVERSITY IN BENGAL, HE WAS HIRED AS AN INTERPRETER BY HAKIM'S FATHER...IS WHAT I IMAGINE.

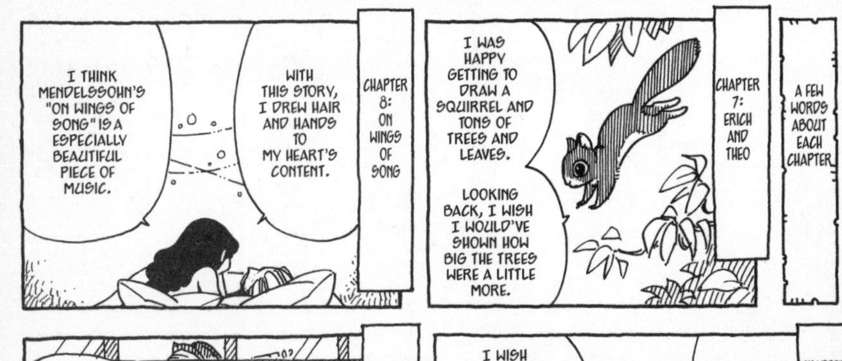
A FEW WORDS ABOUT EACH CHAPTER
CHAPTER 7: ERICH AND THEO
I WAS HAPPY GETTING TO DRAW A SQUIRREL AND TONS OF TREES AND LEAVES.
LOOKING BACK, I WISH I WOULD'VE SHOWN HOW BIG THE TREES WERE A LITTLE MORE.
CHAPTER 8: ON WINGS OF SONG
WITH THIS STORY, I DREW HAIR AND HANDS TO MY HEART'S CONTENT.
I THINK MENDELSSOHN'S "ON WINGS OF SONG" IS A ESPECIALLY BEAUTIFUL PIECE OF MUSIC.

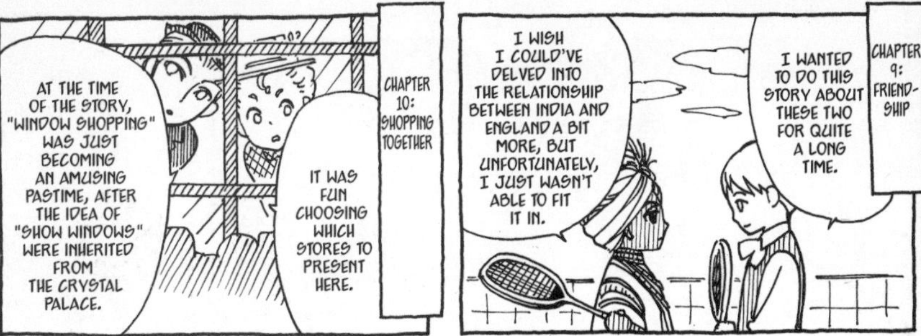
CHAPTER 9: FRIENDSHIP
I WANTED TO DO THIS STORY ABOUT THESE TWO FOR QUITE A LONG TIME.
I WISH I COULD'VE DELVED INTO THE RELATIONSHIP BETWEEN INDIA AND ENGLAND A BIT MORE, BUT UNFORTUNATELY, I JUST WASN'T ABLE TO FIT IT IN.
CHAPTER 10: SHOPPING TOGETHER
IT WAS FUN CHOOSING WHICH STORES TO PRESENT HERE.
AT THE TIME OF THE STORY, "WINDOW SHOPPING" WAS JUST BECOMING AN AMUSING PASTIME, AFTER THE IDEA OF "SHOW WINDOWS" WERE INHERITED FROM THE CRYSTAL PALACE.

CHAPTERS 11 AND 12: 3 SINGERS
MY INTENTION WAS TO DO A LIGHT COMEDY HERE...
...BUT IT KIND OF TURNED INTO A SERIOUS STORY.
THE MAIN CHARACTER HERE IS "ALAN", WHICH REMINDS THAT THERE ARE A LOT OF CHARACTERS IN MY STORIES STARTING WITH "A".
Maybe it's because I like the letter...?
AND THAT'S PRETTY MUCH THE WAY IT WENT.
I HOPE YOU LIKED ONE OR MORE OF THE STORIES ABOVE.

WELL...
THERE'S ONLY ONE MORE EPISODE TO GO TO CONCLUDE THIS "SIDE STORY" SERIES.
EMMA'S STORIES PROPER WILL ALSO END AND I HAVE DEEP EMOTIONS ABOUT IT...
BUT WE HAVE ONE MORE VOLUME TO GO, SO STICK AROUND.
FAREWELL UNTIL THEN.
THE END

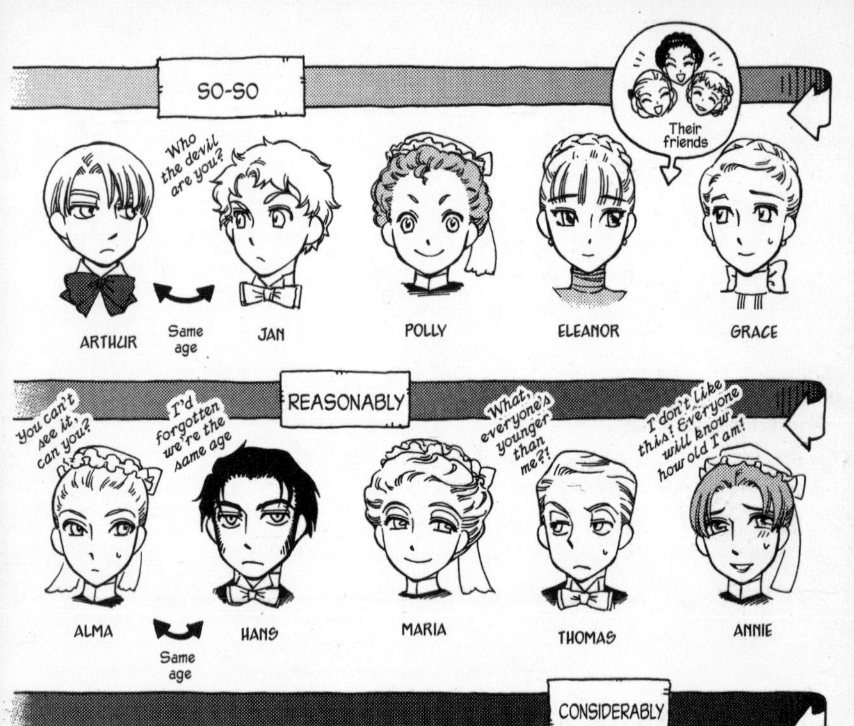

SO-SO
Their friends
Who the devil are you?
ARTHUR
Same age
JAN
POLLY
ELEANOR
GRACE
REASONABLY
You can't see it, can you?
I'd forgotten we're the same age
What, everyone's younger than me?!
I don't like this! Everyone will know how old I am!
ALMA
Same age
HANS
MARIA
THOMAS
ANNIE

CONSIDERABLY

VISCOUNT CAMPBELL

MRS. BEEK

MR. BRUCH

Oh, dear!
Am I that old?
THERESA

OTHERS
Hohoho!
You don't inquire about a lady's age!
ADELE
Age unknown
MONICA
Excluded at her request

CHARACTER AGE RANKING

ACTUALLY, I HAVEN'T DECIDED ON EXACT AGES FOR THE CHARACTERS, SO HERE I'VE ARRANGED THEM ACCORDING TO WHO IS MOST LIKELY OLDER OR YOUNGER THAN WHOM.

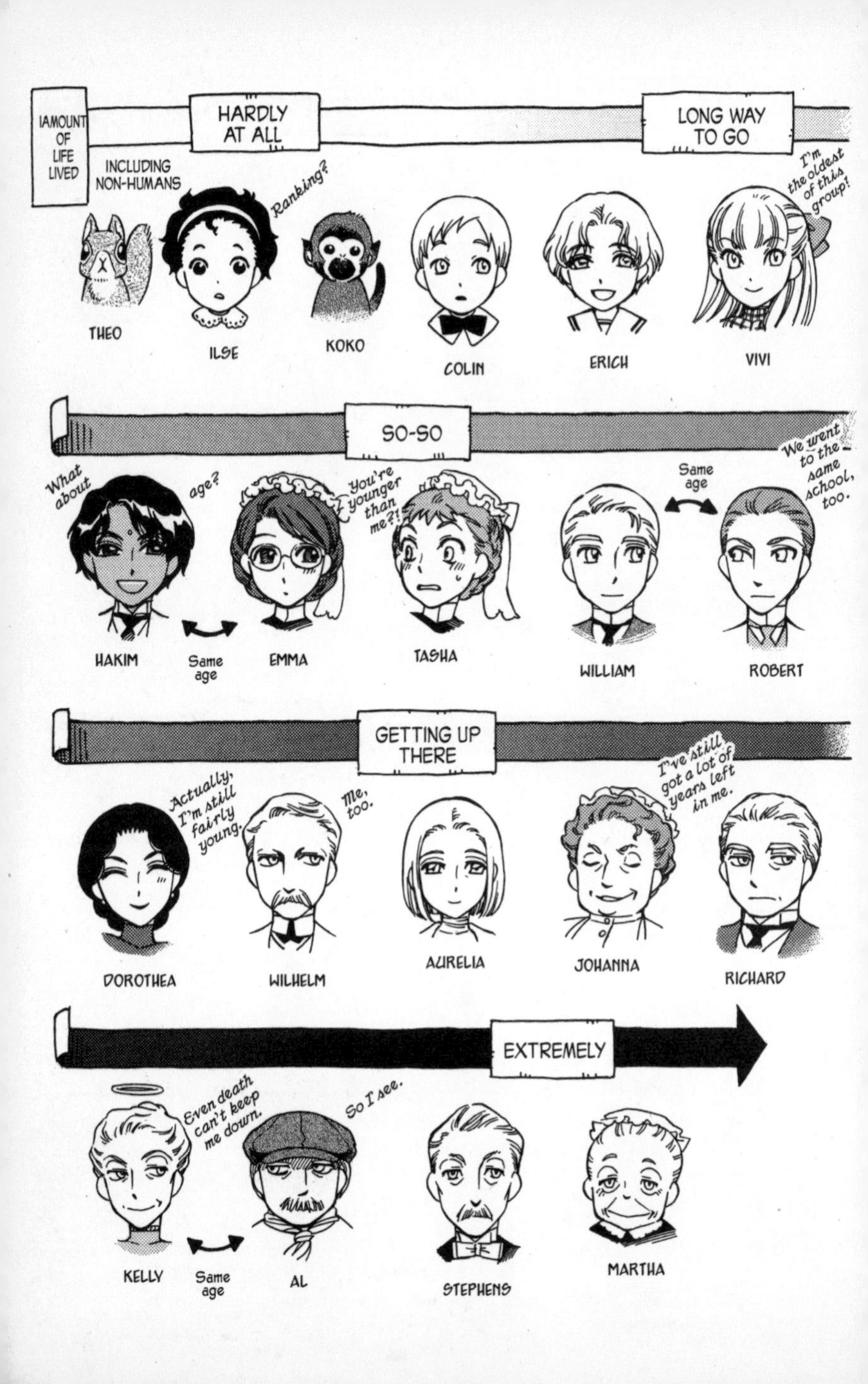

IAMOUNT OF LIFE LIVED
HARDLY AT ALL
LONG WAY TO GO
INCLUDING NON-HUMANS
Ranking?
I'm the oldest of this group!
THEO
ILSE
KOKO
COLIN
ERICH
VIVI
SO-SO
What about
age?
You're younger than me?!
Same age
We went to the same school, too.
HAKIM
Same age
EMMA
TASHA
WILLIAM
ROBERT
GETTING UP THERE
Actually, I'm still fairly young.
Me, too.
I've still got a lot of years left in me.
DOROTHEA
WILHELM
AURELIA
JOHANNA
RICHARD
EXTREMELY
Even death can't keep me down.
So I see.
KELLY
Same age
AL
STEPHENS
MARTHA

DON'T MISS KIICHI'S FINAL ADVENTURE! AVAILABLE NOW!

By Taka Amano. Kiichi has a very important decision to make! An Oni woman tells him it is possible to seal his third horn, which will grow into a tree if unchecked. However, it is this third horn that boosts everyone's skills and keeps Hana from turning back into ink. Unfortunately, all of this power boosting is draining Kiichi's very own life force and could end up killing him. The choice might not be his to make, because the "Researchers" want to capture Kiichi so he'll grow into a giant tree that'll save their world. What is he going to do?!

WHEN KEI FINDS OUT THE TRUTH, WILL SHE BE ABLE TO HANDLE IT? COMING IN AUGUST

TEARS OF A LAMB

Volume 6

By Banri Hidaka. Kei passes all of her exams, but is so consumed with finding out who she was running with the day of the accident that she can't enjoy her scholastic success. When Kanzaki returns from winter break and sees Kei, he makes a passing comment and something goes off inside of her. Kei knows her running partner muttered words just like this, but she just can't remember who it was—or maybe she is too afraid to discover the identity of this mystery accomplice!

KNOW WHAT'S INSIDE

With the wide variety of manga available, CMX understands it can be confusing to determine age-appropriate material. We rate our books in four categories: EVERYONE, TEEN, TEEN + and MATURE. For the TEEN, TEEN + and MATURE categories, we include additional, specific descriptions to assist consumers in determining if the book is age appropriate. (Our MATURE books are shipped shrink-wrapped with a Parental Advisory sticker affixed to the wrapper.)

EVERYONE

Titles with this rating are appropriate for all age readers. They contain no offensive material. They may contain mild violence and/or some comic mischief.

TEEN

Titles with this rating are appropriate for a teen audience and older. They may contain some violent content, language, and/or suggestive themes.

TEEN PLUS

Titles with this rating are appropriate for an audience of 16 and older. They may contain partial nudity, mild profanity and more intense violence.

MATURE

Titles with this rating are appropriate only for mature readers. They may contain graphic violence, nudity, sex and content suitable only for older readers.

This book is manufactured at a facility holding chain-of-custody certification. This paper is made with sustainably managed North American fiber.

Sheldon Drzka – Translation and Adaptation
Janice Chiang – Lettering
Larry Berry – Design
Sarah Farber – Assistant Editor
Jim Chadwick – Editor

ISBN: 978-1-4012-2071-6

All the pages in this book were created—and are printed here—in Japanese RIGHT-to-LEFT format. No artwork has been reversed or altered, so you can read the stories the way the creators meant for them to be read.

RIGHT TO LEFT?!

Traditional Japanese manga starts at the upper right-hand corner, and moves right-to-left as it goes down the page. Follow this guide for an easy understanding.